MOZART AND MASONRY

Da Capo Press Music Reprint Series

GENERAL EDITOR

FREDERICK FREEDMAN

VASSAR COLLEGE

MOZART

and

MASONRY

by

PAUL NETTL

 DA CAPO PRESS • NEW YORK • 1970

A Da Capo Press Reprint Edition

This Da Capo Press edition of Paul Nettl's
Mozart and Masonry is an unabridged republication
of the first edition published in New York in 1957.
It is reprinted by special arrangement with the Philosophical Library, Inc.

Library of Congress Catalog Card Number 78-114564

SBN 306-71922-3

Published by Da Capo Press
A Division of Plenum Publishing Corporation
227 West 17th Street, New York, N.Y. 10011

Manufactured in the United States of America

MOZART AND MASONRY

MOZART

and

MASONRY

by

PAUL NETTL

PHILOSOPHICAL LIBRARY

NEW YORK

Printed in the United States of America

To

HERMAN B WELLS

President, Indiana University

CONTENTS

List of Illustrations

INTRODUCTION

INTRODUCTION

A MONG INTELLECTUAL FORCES of the eighteenth century, based
as they were on the veneration and exaltation of nature and
man, none is of such fundamental importance as Freemasonry. It
is significant because it combined all of the humanitarian teachings
of its time, systematized them, illustrated them with symbols, and
made them generally available in a coherent organization. One
occasionally encounters the belief that Freemasonry has purely historical value today, that it is simply a dead or dying branch of the
great humanitarian movement in the Age of Reason which has
persisted through inertia. If this were so, the flowering which has
characterized Freemasonry since the second World War would be
inexplicable and we would expect to find only meager remains of
it, similar to those of the Rosicrucians and the Illuminati. But as
a matter of fact, a new wave of Freemasonry has been emanating
from the United States. Masonic lodges, which declined in importance during the nineteenth century, are regaining the positions
they held during the eighteenth. For the ideal of humanitarianism
makes men associate in one way or another, especially after great
catastrophes. The wars of the seventeenth and eighteenth centuries, fought primarily for the interests of the ruling classes, the
measures of suppression of that period, and the French Revolution,
all these resulted in a desire for humanitarian thinking. And the
same process can be observed in our time.

One of the chief attractions of Freemasonry is the example set
by many great intellectuals of the eighteenth century. Among the
ardent Masons were Goethe, Lessing, Wieland, Fichte, and Frederick the Great. By the end of the eighteenth century there were
few important figures who had not been strongly affected by that
new movement.

What then is Freemasonry, and what are its purposes? The un-
informed usually assume it is a secret society with some kind of
political aim augmented by a mysterious ritual. Forced to meet in

secrecy in many countries (Germany, Austria, Russia, Italy, etc.), the Freemasons inspired a whole set of fantastic stories which revolved about their activities. Since the members rarely broke their reserve even to defend themselves against false and humiliating accusations, some people equated their silence with wickedness and this attitude is still with us. The mystic symbols, the ritual which makes use of prehistoric customs and ancient Near Eastern mythology has contributed to it. Because of its secrecy, the Nazi and communist governments suppressed Masonry by every possible means. One may recall that in the nineteenth century certain Roman Catholic groups spread the story that Mozart had been poisoned by Freemasons. Among various "explanatory" writings is a book, *Freemasonry*, by Schwartz-Bostunitsch which purports to enlighten people about the aims of the order. It represents Freemasonry as a secret Jewish society which, under the command of the Learned Elders of Zion, works toward world domination. It is only a short step from there to the anti-semitic and anti-Masonic outpourings in the Nazi periodical *Stürmer*. Attention should also be called to a polemical pamphlet by Mathilde Ludendorff, *Die ungesühnten Frevel an Luther, Schiller, Lessing und Mozart* (The unexpiated outrages against Luther, Schiller, Lessing, and Mozart). She claims in deadly earnest that Mozart was poisoned by his fellow-Masons because of his pro-German views.

Secrecy is not the key to Freemasonry. Everything concerning its aims and its ritual is available to the public in books and manuals. Indeed, some well-informed outsiders know more about the Craft than many a mason of lower degree who should not have and does not wish any premature knowledge. Masonry keeps no secrets from the uninitiated! Yet there is a masonic secret, a mystery, an experience that cannot be taught or explained because it lies, like every mystic experience, beyond the realm of controlled consciousness. At its deepest level it is identical with intense feeling and empathy. The secret of Freemasonry is the secret of experiencing true love for all mankind, a positive attitude towards man and life, and broad affirmation of God. It is the realization that beyond the dark and material world there is a realm of light towards which all men must strive. The peculiarity of Masonry is its symbolism, with its roots in the distant past, intensifying this experience whose sensuous aspect lies in the beauty of the ritual.

Masonry officially enters history with the founding of the first

4

Grand Lodge of London on June 24, 1717, but it is descended from the stone-masons' guilds of the Middle Ages. The prefix "free" signifies freedom from joining a guild and, in a broader sense, hints at the speculative masonry which arose from the active masonry. During the seventeenth century more and more persons of high moral standing were accepted into the lodges.

Freemasons work to build the Temple of Humanity, symbolized by King Solomon's temple; hence the name "royal art." Ritual and vocabulary are taken from the old masonic guilds which, like other guilds, created their own body of legends. (For example, Hiram, Solomon's architect, is killed by three murderers because he refuses to divulge the secret.) Elements of ancient Near Eastern mysteries and some elements of Rosicrucian thinking were woven into the Hiramic legend, resulting in an emphasis on secrecy. During the eighteenth century a strong rationalistic flavor, favorable to all charitable, humanitarian, and international ideas, was added. Freemasonry has not remained unified and static since the eighteenth century. Its face has changed along with shifting intellectual trends.

The eighteenth century is considered the pinnacle of Masonic development. In England and France Freemasonry already had a social character along with its moral and ethical sides. During the Age of Reason, many of the ablest men in Europe joined its ranks, largely aristocrats and, to a lesser extent, philosophers and poets. A number of heads of state belonged to the Craft, for example Frederick II, Frederick William II, Grand Duke Carl August of Weimar, Emperor Francis I, George IV of England, George Washington, and most presidents of the United States after him. German philosophy was represented by Fichte and Krause, literature by Bürger, Chamisso, Claudius, Kleist, Klopstock, Wieland, Herder, and, above all, Goethe, whose works drew heavily from Masonry. Lessing made a significant contribution to masonic literature in his dialogues *Ernst und Falk.* Pope, Sterne, and Swift were among the ablest masonic writers in Britain, as were Beaumarchais, Stendhal, and most of the Encyclopedists in France. But most important for the intellectual history of Masonry is Mozart, because the *Magic Flute,* one of the greatest art works of all time, was the direct result of his Masonic associations. The intellectual greats among the Masons felt themselves members not only of the spiritual but also of the actual nobility since they associated on brotherly terms with members of the aristocracy and with worldly potentates.

Much has been written about the relationships between various phases of culture and Freemasonry. Ferdinand Schneider described the influence of Masonry on German thinking during the end of the eighteenth century and has shown that the roots of romanticism can be found in its more mystical offshoots, the Illuminati and the Rosicrucians. Entire bodies of literature were profoundly influenced by Masonry, possibly because of its curious mixture of free-thinking and rationalism, materialism and a kind of mysticism which occasionally approached Crypto-Catholicism. "Strict observance" was supposedly linked with the Jesuits.

But in the last analysis we have the same situation today as 150 years ago; a world-view basically Christian is practiced, accompanied by mystic symbols. Presumably this has a special attraction for soft, vacillating individuals. A person like Lessing was attracted to the ethical rationalism of Masonry, while Goethe sceptically viewed the combination of these principles. Mozart, finally, was more inclined to its mysticism. This can be felt with certainty after hearing the gentle, mysterious sounds of the *Magic Flute* and the *Masonic Funeral Music*.

MOZART AND MASONRY

MOZART AND THE CRAFT

Mozart's association with Freemasonry did not begin with his initiation in Vienna, for already during his Salzburg days many influences and events pointed him towards it. In order to understand Masonic conditions in Salzburg at that time, we should glance at neighboring Munich, the center of persecution of the Illuminati, then rampant in Southern Germany.

In 1784 the Elector issued a decree banning all secret societies in Bavaria. After several protests by Freemasons and Illuminati, Father Frank and Kreittmayr, in the name of Elector Carl Theodor, issued a prohibition on March 2, 1785, which resulted in the banishment of Weisshaupt, the "pope" of the Illuminati, from Ingolstadt. Further measures against this group followed on June 9 and August 16. Some high officials, including Count Pappenheim and Chancellor von Löwendahl, were not pursued because they had connections at court. Others, notably the physician, Professor Bader, Master of the Lodge in Munich, received the full impact of persecution. Bader's lodge was a daughter lodge of the "Royal York." It had been elevated on August 20, 1781, to manager of affairs in Bavaria and Italy, and co-manager in Switzerland, Sweden, and Franconia. It had its own system, based on that used by the "Chevaliers bien-faisants" in Lyons. Some time later, on July 3, 1783, Bader joined the Eclectic Lodge.

The order of the Illuminati was founded in the 1770's. Their "pope," Weisshaupt, used the Jesuits as a model for his organization. In 1776 he founded a secret order in Ingolstadt called the Perfectibilists, whose purpose was to "unite all men capable of independent thought, unobstructed by vested interests, irrespective of their nationality, position, or religion, to work for a lofty purpose." They were going to turn mankind into a "masterpiece of reason and, thus, to attain the highest perfection in the art of government."

Weisshaupt himself had been brought up by the Jesuits in

Ingolstadt. The internal organization of the order was along Masonic lines and each member was given a special name. Weisshaupt chose the name Spartacus. The founders, who included Lori, secretary of the Bavarian state lottery, and Dr. Bader, were known as Areopagites. In 1779 Weisshaupt evolved a syllabus which provided for three degrees—Novice, Minerval, and Enlightened Minerval—in the manner of the blue St. John's Masonry. Weisshaupt found an eager supporter in Baron von Knigge. In its prime, the order had over 2,000 members, among them Carl August of Weimar, Ernst and August of Gotha, Herder, Pestalozzi, and Goethe (who had the name Abaris). Joseph von Sonnenfels and Mozart's friend Ignaz von Born were important members in Vienna. Soon the order had also made bitter enemies, among them some groups of Freemasons, but especially the Jesuits. Elector Carl Theodor of Bavaria, influenced by his Father Confessor, the Rosicrucian Frank, ordered the elimination of all secret societies. Persecutions and arrests soon set in, officers and civil servants losing their positions. Fantastic rumors were spread about the order, accusing it of murders, poisonings, conspiracies to dominate the world, and all other imaginable crimes. Though membership was punishable by death, Ernst von Gotha gave asylum to the Illuminati. Finally Count von Stollberg, who had taken over the leadership of the group from Weisshaupt, limited its activities. In 1785 the Minerval Church in Weimar, under the direction of the writer and composer of military music, Christoph Bode, was the last to close its doors. Bode, a true rationalist and a friend of Goethe's, was a member of the musical circle of Weimar. In 1788 Goethe wrote to Carl August from Florence that the Swiss composer Kayser was intending to copy some church music by Palestrina, Morales, and Scarlatti and bring it to Weimar, adding, in jest, "if only Bode does not hear of this." He seemed to fear that the zealous enlightener would fly into a rage, in the belief that these Catholic melodies might draw the weaker-spirited into popish superstition.

Beginning in 1783 there had existed in Salzburg an Eclectic Lodge, "Zur Fürsicht" (Prudence) under the direction of Count Spaur.[1] Several of the members belonged to both the Salzburg and the Munich lodges. Koch also says that Leopold and Wolfgang Mozart were Visiting Members of the Eclectic Lodge in Salzburg. Apart from this there were two Illuminati lodges—"Apollo" and

"Wissenschaft" (knowledge), as well as a ladies' "Adoptionsloge."

Koch also mentions the Counts Franz and Nepomuk Spaur, Professor Schelle, Count Wolfegg, Lorenz Hübner (the Salzburg topographer and editor of the *Oberdeutsche Literaturzeitung*), the court councillors Ernst and Franz Gilowsky, Rector P. Korbinian Gärtner of the university, and the musicians Brindl and Benedikt Hacker as members of these lodges. Mozart was friendly with Wolfegg and, on October 24, 1777, he wrote from Augsburg that this count had attended a concert of his and had otherwise taken him under his patronage. Wolfegg's name frequently appears in Mozart's correspondence, as do those of Spaur and Gilowsky. "Katherl" Gilowsky seems to have especially appealed to him. Basil Amman was another friend of Mozart's among the Illuminati. He died insane at the age of 29 and Mozart wrote on June 7, 1783, ironically commenting on his friend's mental state: "I am sorry about Basil, and I would never have expected this of him. . . . If you should be able to obtain a German song composed by him, be so good as to send it to me; it might make me laugh. . . ."

Of the two Illuminati musicians, Brindl and Hacker, the former's name appears in a letter of Mozart's written to his sister on October 28, 1772. Mozart refers to him as the "Amant" of Nannerl Nader, a childhood friend of Mozart and his sister.

Hacker is not mentioned in the correspondence. Born in Deppendorf, Bavaria, in 1769, he established a music store in Salzburg in 1802. He wrote a short opera, *List gegen List, oder der Teufel im Waldschloss* (Tit for tat, or the devil at the hunting-lodge) and drawing-room songs for part-singing. Apparently he was interested in folklore, having collected songs in the Alps (Gay songs from the "crazy Alps"). Eitner[2] indicates that several of his masses were found in the library of the Gesellschaft der Musikfreunde in Vienna, but Librarian Poll disposed of them for lack of space. Apparently neither Leopold nor Wolfgang Mozart left any written evidence of their membership in the lodges of the Illuminati.

Leopold wrote a letter to his daughter on October 14, 1785, which casts doubt on his membership in the Illuminati. Of the persons mentioned in it, Christian Cannabich and Friedrich Ramm, the famous Mannheim oboist, are well known. (14.10.1785)

11

"As I started to write, Herr Rahm and young Cannabich came in to see me. They are going to Italy. And as Le Brun and his wife just now happen to be in Verona, where she is singing in an opera, and two pipers are too many for one inn, Rahm is going to Graz and then to Venice by way of Trieste.

"I had to take him to call on Count Lützow. They will stay until tomorrow, unless they are asked to perform at court, because Countess Schönborn is also here; she and Count Guntecker. But Count Baar has left. On the other hand, Count Clam, the aimant of Madame Duschek (from Prague) is also here. Well, we shall see what happens. You may have heard that Dr. Hutterer was taken to the fortress by five men eight days ago at seven o'clock in the evening. For how long? They say for an indefinite period. Even Profos Rieder is supposed to go there for four months—or perhaps he is already there—because he sent Guttmann some papers, or had him send them—nobody knows for sure. From Rahm, and already from Marchand's letters, I learned that not even one-hundredth of the rumors told here about the Illuminati in Munich is true. The investigations were quite proper. Some obstinate ones were sent away or went of their own accord. The rest, who made a clean breast of it to the Elector, remained—even one of their heads, Dr. Bader. The funny thing is that a list of the members of Bader's lodge is circulating here, some 70 persons, many of them high-ranking priests, among them Count Spaur, the Canon of Salzburg. According to Herr Rahm, the true Masons, of whom the Elector is one, are very much aroused about these peculiar people. That is why this gossip was thoroughly investigated."

At the time Mozart was admitted to those circles in Vienna which were largely composed of Freemasons, the number of lodges was large. After the accession of Joseph II, to be sure, some restrictions were imposed. A decree of December 11, 1785 limited the number of lodges in capital cities to three and commanded them to submit detailed lists of members from time to time for the inspection of the government. Nevertheless, the reign of Joseph II constitutes the beginning of a glorious chapter in the history of Austrian Freemasonry. The splintering of the order into several branches may have been the reason for this close supervision. There had appeared a number of rather doubtful systems which carried on all sorts of shady business and quackery in the

name of Freemasonry, as witness the flagrant case of Cagliostro.
No wonder, therefore, that preventive measures had to be taken in
order to preserve the health of the movement. Around 1781 the
following lodges were operating in Vienna: "Zur wahren Eintracht" (true harmony), a daughter lodge of "Zur gekrönten
Hoffnung" (crowned hope), "Zum Palmbaum" (palm tree),
"Zum heiligen Joseph" (St. Joseph), "Zur Beständigkeit" (stead-
fastness), "Zu den drei Adlern" (three eagles), and "Zu den
drei Feuern" (three fires). In the "True Harmony" lodge some of
the greatest and most brilliant men of the time were gathered
under the leadership of the famous Ignaz von Born. He was the
second Master, having previously been active in Prague, where he
had revived the lodge "Zu den drei gekrönten Säulen" (the three
crowned pillars).

In the *Josephinische Curiosa,* Born is described as follows:
"One of the most remarkable, active, meritorious, and immortal
men of the Josephinian period, he was highly esteemed, decorated,
and treated as a friend by the Emperor." Born hoped to establish
a kind of Masonic academy in Vienna, based on freedom of
thought and conscience, similar to the "Neuf Soeurs" in Paris.
It was not long before the best intellects of Vienna and Austria
joined his lodge. Pezzl says of him: "I know of no one whom
people would rather meet, or hear with greater interest. He rules
unchallenged in the best society without causing displeasure. He
has not written much, but everything he says should be published,
for it is always witty, relevant, and his satire is without insult.
All of this knowledge and wisdom is uttered so spontaneously and
playfully that it sounds like ordinary common sense. His utter-
ances are so unique and distinctive that he uncovers unsuspected
slants on even the most commonplace matters. All that enters his
wonderful memory is retained. He has read and investigated
everything from Church Fathers to fairy tales."

Besides Born, a number of other important intellectuals were
members of the new lodge: Alois Blumauer, Joseph Franz Ratschky, Leon, Retzer, Johann Baptist Alxinger, Bergmann; and
the scholars Denis, Gruber, Haidinger, Herrmann, Märter, Johann
Mayer, Joseph Mayer, Menz, Müller, Pacassi, Pallas, Ployer, Raab,
Ruprecht, Schrank, Unterberger, Voigt; the custodian of the university library, Carl Joseph Michaeler, a Catholic priest who became a Freemason in spite of the papal bull against the order and

who wrote an excellent polemic against his clerical adversaries; Professor of philosophy Groag; Anton Sauter; Count Ayala; Hilchenbach, the superintendent of the Protestant community in Austria; Schmutzer, director of the Academy of Engravings; Schiller's friend Reinhold, who had to flee to Weimar because of his progressive views, and who married Wieland's daughter, contributor to the literary journal *Teutscher Merkur* and later professor of philosophy in Jena. Other famous members were Stütz, director of the Imperial Natural History Collection; Georg Forster, who circumnavigated the globe; Franz Zauner, a sculptor, creator of the equestrian statue of Joseph II and the monument at the tomb of Leopold II; the engraver Adam; the publisher Artaria; Leber, physician to the Empress Maria Theresia, who also taught at the university; Peter Jordan; Franz Jäger, the physicist. Of considerable importance also was Angelo Soliman,[3] the "noble Negro," an African prince who played an important part in the social life of Vienna and is never missing from the roll of the lodge. I have mentioned all of these individuals in order to give a detailed impression of the Masonic environment of Mozart.

Today we know all the details of Mozart's entry into the Craft. To be sure, he left no written record of his Masonic associations and it is generally assumed that either he, his wife, or his father destroyed all such papers. This may have been done out of fear of Colloredo, Archbishop of Salzburg, with whom Mozart had several disagreements, and perhaps also because of an anti-Masonic movement which set in after Joseph's death.

The Viennese Brother Kulka and Otto Erich Deutsch have done research on Mozart's admission and membership. They studied the documents of the lodge "Zur wahren Eintracht," preserved at the State Archives, and came to the conclusion that Mozart was admitted to the lodge "Zur Wohltätigkeit" and not, as had been supposed by such earlier biographers as Hermann Abert, into the lodge "Zur gekrönten Hoffnung." Because of the above-mentioned restrictions imposed by the emperor, these two lodges had been united with some others to form the lodge "Zur neugekrönten Hoffnung" (newly crowned hope). His admission was presumably arranged by Baron von Gemmingen, the Master of the lodge whose acquaintance Mozart had made in Mannheim. Gemmingen (1755-1836) was the author of *Mannheimische Dramaturgie* (1779) and a play, *Der deutsche Hausvater* (1780; The German head of the house). His name appears frequently in Mozart's letters. On November 18, 1785, Leopold Mozart wrote to his daughter: "Soon you will be able to obtain in Salzburg the beautiful book by my very good friend Baron von Gemmingen, which has already been published in Vienna." Wolfgang Mozart wanted to compose a melodrama on Gemmingen's *Semiramis*. In Vienna the Baron published the *Magazin für Wissenschaft und Kunst* (magazine for science and art) from 1784 to 1785. His secretary Leopold Aloys Hoffmann was at first an eager Freemason and enlightener who later assumed the role of Judas and became notorious for his attacks on the order.

Until recently, the year 1785 had been accepted as the time of Mozart's initiation, but according to the studies of Kulka, it appears that Mozart was initiated into the lodge "Zur Wohltätigkeit" on December 14, 1784. Also initiated at this meeting was Wenzel Summer, chaplain in Erdberg. Mozart had been proposed for membership on December 5, 1784 and became no. 20 in the lodge register. On December 24, 1784, he paid an official visit to the lodge "Zur wahren Eintracht" (true harmony) before being passed to the second degree at the request of his mother lodge. This ceremony took place on January 7, 1785, at the 343rd meeting of the lodge "Zur wahren Eintracht." The entry into the minutes of this meeting says: "After the lodge was opened in the first and second degrees two entered apprentices were passed to the second degree with the usual ceremony. They were Vincenz Marquis Canarisi, son of Joseph, 34 years old, born in Como in Austrian Lombardy, Captain in the Royal-Imperial Regiment Belgioso at the request of the very worshipful lodge 'Zur aufgehenden Sonne' (rising sun) in Brünn; and Brother Wolfgang Mozard (sic), at the request of the very worshipful lodge 'Zur Wohltätigkeit.' "

In the minutes of the next meeting of the lodge "Zur wahren Eintracht," Mozart's name is not mentioned, but Haydn's appears. According to the minutes, it was proposed "to initiate the Petitioner Joseph Haydn, music director to Prince Esterhazy, also the Petitioner Baron Hallberg of Brussels." After being balloted on January 24, Haydn was initiated into the lodge "Zur wahren Eintracht" on February 11, 1785. However, the minutes indicate that "the ballot was unanimously in favor of the candidates and their initiation was arranged for January 28." Mozart appeared at the meeting of the 28th, probably to greet his venerated friend as a brother mason, but the initiation did not take place as Haydn was prevented from coming. At the 353rd meeting, "the Petitioner Haydn was exempted from paying dues and his initiation set for February 11." At the next meeting, on that date, he was presented and accepted as the "Petitioner Joseph Haydn, son of Mathias, 51 years old, born on May 1, of Roman Catholic faith, a commoner, born in Rohrau in Austria, by occupation music director to Prince Esterhazy."

Haydn's initiation into the lodge "Zur wahren Eintracht" was presumably delegated by the lodge "Zur Wahrheit." He seems to have attended only once, although he wrote a letter to Count Apponyi on February 2, 1785, from Esterhaz: "Yesterday I received a letter from my future sponsor, Baron von Webern. He writes that he waited for me in vain last Friday, when my initiation, to which I am anxiously looking forward, was to have taken place. Through the negligence of our hussars I did not receive the invitation in time and the ceremony was postponed to next Friday (not February 4, as Abafi[4] says, but February 11). Oh, how I wish it were that Friday already. Oh, to feel the unspeakable joy of being among such worthy men!"

After the initiation, the Junior Warden, Joseph von Holzmeister, addressed Haydn on the subject of harmony. In spite of the composer's great longing to belong to the Craft, he seems to have lost interest in it after his entry, or possibly his heavy duties prevented his making the trip to Vienna.

Mozart attended two further meetings, on January 14 and 28. On March 28 it was announced in the lodge "Zur Wohltätigkeit" that the music director, Leopold Mozart, and Bashy had been proposed as candidates for initiation. "Since both are about to leave the city, we have applied for dispensation in their behalf." Dispensation was applied for on April 1 and granted by the Grand Lodge of Vienna, but there are no minutes which directly record Leopold's initiation. It took place on April 6, 1785, and ten days later, on April 16, Leopold had already been passed to the second degree.

The minutes read: "Brother and member of the worshipful lodge 'Zur Wohltätigkeit' Leopold Mozart was passed to the second degree with the usual ceremony." On April 22, both father and son were again present, and at that meeting Leopold was already raised to the third degree. The entry says: "The Master announces that, at the request of the very worshipful lodge 'Zur Wohltätigkeit,' the Fellow Craft Leopold Mozard (sic), member of the lodge 'Zur Wohltätigkeit,' son of Johann Georg, was raised to the third degree."

Mozart attended the lodge "Zur wahren Eintracht" on August 12 and again, for the last time, on December 19, 1785. At this last meeting of the year Freiherr von Hornstein was initiated and Otto von Gemmingen, the Master of Mozart's mother lodge, was present.

On February 11 at one P.M., Leopold Mozart had arrived at 846 Schulerstrasse (now no. 8) where his son lived on the first floor. Haydn visited the Mozarts the very next day, one day after his initiation. In his company were the Barons Bartholomeus and Anton von Tinti, who had been initiated with Haydn. The string quartets K.458, K.464, and K.465 were performed that evening, and Haydn made a remark which has since become famous: "I declare to you before God, as an honest man, that your son is the greatest composer I know either personally or by reputation. He has taste as well as a consummate knowledge of the art of composition."

We have the impression that on this occasion Wolfgang Mozart and Haydn discussed the possibility of Leopold's initiation into Freemasonry. It almost looks as if Wolfgang had complained to Papa Haydn about the estrangement between himself and his father, and had suggested Leopold's initiation as a remedy. If that is the case, their hopes were not fulfilled, for even after his initiation, Leopold could not forgive his son for having married Constanze Weber. It appears from his letters to his daughter that Leopold was very anxious to return to Salzburg. His return seems to have been delayed because he was to be raised to the third degree on April 22, at a ceremony at which Ignaz von Born served as Master. Leopold left Vienna three days later, and on April 30 he wrote to his daughter from Linz:

"I am writing on an impulse and I hope you will receive this. I finally left Vienna on the 25th at 10:30 in company of your brother and his wife. At Burkerstorf we ate together at noon, then they returned to Vienna." Of course Leopold Mozart kept his Masonic activities completely secret. There are no hints of them in the letters to his son, or to his daughter who was now married

17

to Baron Berchtold zu Sonnenburg, a curator at near-by St. Gilgen. On June 2, only two months after being raised by Born, he wrote to his daughter: "Baron von Born arrived in the evening at the inn and immediately went to call on the prince. He was invited for dinner the next day, and the poet Blumauer, who accompanied him, was asked to coffee after dinner. Then they continued their journey to Gastein, and will not stop here again until their return trip." Both Born and Blumauer, the famous Austrian poet, had been present at Leopold's raising. Was it the strict observance of Masonic secrecy that sealed the lips of the otherwise talkative Leopold, or was it fear of the archbishop?

Among Masonic documents in the Austrian State Archives, Otto Erich Deutsch found several invitations to concerts arranged by the lodges in Vienna. On April 20, 1785 at 6:30 lodges "Zu den drei Adlern" and "Zum Palmbaum" invited the other lodges to a concert at which Brothers Mozart and Anton Stadler performed. After the concert Brother Mozart was to entertain the audience "with his popular improvisations." It was a benefit for two fellow-Masons, the brilliant clarinettists Anton David from Offenburg near Strassburg, and Vincent Springer from Jungbunzlau near Prague. Both were also masters of the basset-horn. Perhaps Mozart's acquaintance with these two artists is responsible for his preference for this instrument in many of his later works.

On December 15 the lodge "Zur gekrönten Hoffnung" arranged a concert with a truly gargantuan program: a symphony by Brother Paul Wranitzky, director of music to Count Esterhazy; a duet-concerto for basset-horn by Brothers David and Springer; the cantata *Maurerfreude* (K. 471) and a piano concerto by Mozart; a serenade by Stadler for six wind instruments in which Brother Theodor Lotz, violist and first clarinettist of the Batthyany band in Bratislava, played contra-bassoon; another symphony by Wranitzky, composed especially for the lodge. After all this, Mozart began his improvisations. We are not certain which piano concerto was performed on this occasion, but it may have been K. 467 in C major, Mozart's most recently completed one, or K. 482 in E flat major, which he finished the next day.

Both the lodges "Zur wahren Eintracht" and "Zur Wohltätigkeit" met at that time at the house of Joseph von Weinbrenner, "Zum roten Krebsen" (red crayfish) in the Pressgasse at the center of Vienna. Mozart apparently was acquainted with Weinbren-

18

ner, whose name appears as one of the subscribers to the February-Academy of 1784. (In Schiedermair's edition of Mozart's letters the name is incorrectly given as Joseph de Weinbremes.)

It is quite interesting to trace the few indications of Mozart's Masonic associations through his correspondence. The character of Sarastro in the *Magic Flute* is usually assumed to be modelled on Ignaz von Born. But his name appears only once, and also in a list of subscribers to an Academy concert sent by Mozart to his father on March 20, a list containing a number of well-known Freemasons. The only other Masonic references are in his letters to the Viennese merchant Michael Puchberg, addressed as "dearest brother," "esteemed brother in the Craft," and signed "brother" or "friend and brother." It was Puchberg who often came to Mozart's financial aid. In 1777, Puchberg had become a member of the lodge "Zu den drei Adlern" and later he joined the lodge "Zum Palmbaum." He played a major financial role in the former and it is evident that he underwrote the above-mentioned concert. Puchberg's first wife was the widow of his former employer Michael Saliet, who is mentioned in a Mozart letter of August 21, 1773, indicating that Mozart and Puchberg must have been acquainted at that early date. In 1784, Puchberg was married again, this time to Anna Eckart.

Mozart's famous letters to Puchberg give us a clear picture of his unhappy financial situation, especially desperate after 1788. Puchberg helped him on several occasions, but some biographers have blamed him for not seeing his way clear to give Mozart the really substantial loan he was hoping for, only continuing to help him with comparatively small sums. In defense against this accusation, motivated by anti-Masonic feeling, we must point out that Puchberg was only too well aware of the vagaries of the Mozart couple. He could exercise a certain amount of control by giving them only a little at a time. When Mozart died his debt to Puchberg had grown to 1000 gulden and of course all claims for repayment were waived. Puchberg then became the guardian of Mozart's two children, Karl and Wolfgang. A moving letter from Haydn, written from London shortly after Mozart's death, shows how Puchberg cared for the composer's estate:

"I was quite beside myself for a considerable time after hearing the news of his death, and could not believe that providence had so soon recalled so irreplaceable a man into the other world. I only regret that he failed to convince the still unenlightened Englishmen of what I preach to them daily. . . . Be so good, dear friend, as to send me a list of the works which are still unknown here. I shall do my utmost to further them in the best interests of the widow. I wrote the poor woman three weeks ago in order to tell her that when her dear son is old enough I shall give him free lessons in composition to the best of my power so that his father will be replaced to some degree."

An undated letter of Mozart's, previously published by Schiedermair, contains apologies for missing a lodge meeting:

"Dear Brother, I returned home an hour ago with a bad headache and cramps in my stomach. I have been hoping for improvement, but I am afraid there is no sign of it, and I can see that I am not destined to be present at today's solemn celebration. I beg you, therefore, dear brother, to present my apologies. The greatest loss will be mine.

> *I am for ever,*
> *Your sincere*
> BROTHER MOZART."

Mozart probably cultivated some Masonic associations in Prague. It is significant that on the occasion of his visit there in January, 1787, the first to welcome him should have been Count Canal, the moving spirit behind the founding of the lodge "Zur Wahrheit und Einigkeit" (truth and unity). Mozart wrote to Jaquin on January 15, 1787, describing some of the important events in the early part of his stay in Prague. At Count Canal's house he dined and attended an opera by Paisiello. He visited Pater Ungar, head of the university library, who was also a member of the new lodge of which Canal was the Senior and Ungar the Junior Warden. Another member, Gottlieb August Meissner, reports that Mozart visited the lodge several times towards the end of his stay. According to apocryphal reports *(Rococobilder)* by his grandson Alfred Meissner, Gottlieb August Meissner, who made notes of the most important events in contemporary Prague, was a member of the lodge "Zur Wahrheit und Einigkeit." He reveals that the brethren formed a guard of honor and welcomed Mozart by singing his cantata *Maurerfreude,* which he had composed in 1785 in honor of Born. This consideration moved Mozart deeply. Thanking them, he said that he would pay homage to Masonry in a better way in the near future. He was referring to the *Magic Flute* which was already taking shape in his mind.

In his book, *Br. Mozart, Freimaurer und Illuminaten*, Koch describes a document said to be in the Salzburger Museum. He believes it to be Mozart's Lodge Certificate. It is in French:

"We, the Grand Master, the Deputy Master, the Wardens, officers, and members of the just and perfect lodge 'Crowned Hope' situated in the Orient of Vienna in Austria, make it known that we recognize the venerable Brother as an Entered Apprentice, Fellow Craft, and free and accepted Master Mason, and a member of our Lodge. And we recommend our aforesaid Brother to our good Brethren, united and dispersed over the face of the earth. Given at the lodge 'Crowned Hope' in the Orient of Vienna in Austria, March 22, Anno Lucis 5792." It is hard to find a reason for Koch's acceptance of this document, for Mozart's name is not even mentioned.

A letter from Mozart's widow to the music publishing house Breitkopf & Härtel, written in 1800, is of interest here: "You know that my husband was a Freemason. . . . he also wanted to found a society to be called *Grotte* (the grotto). I found a fragment of an essay about it and gave it to someone who knew about it and thus might be able to complete it. . . . I am herewith sending you an essay to help you with your biography. It is largely in my husband's own handwriting and is about an order or a society which he wanted to found, to be called 'The Grotto.' I cannot furnish any more information about it. The elder Stadler, court clarinettist, wrote the rest of the essay and could probably explain it. He is reluctant to admit this knowledge because secret orders and societies are so much hated nowadays."

It is not known exactly what kind of a society this "Grotto" was to have been. Mozart may have envisaged a merry secret society similar to the *Ludlamshöhle* (Ludlam's cave) which was founded in 1810 by Castelli and Mozart's brother-in-law Joseph Lange. (The essay by Mozart and Stadler is unfortunately unknown to me.)

Little is known of Mozart's Masonic activities during the last years of his life. It is the period of the Puchberg letters, but it is also the time when he was composing the *Magic Flute*. Freemasonry has often been accused of neglecting Mozart when he was poor and ill, for it has been pointed out that there was not even enough money for his personal grave. It was not the Masons, of course, but Constanze who, on the advice of the famous Van Swieten, ordered a third class funeral for her husband which meant burial in a grave for four corpses.[5] Van Swieten, Salieri, Süssmayr, and a few non-Masonic friends attended the funeral. However, at the next meeting of the lodge "Zur gekrönten Hoffnung," the new name of "Zur neugekrönten Hoffnung," a memorial meeting was held along with a raising ceremony. Brother Hensler delivered a funeral oration.[6] The words of this oration were printed by Brother Ignaz Alberti in 1792; an excerpt follows:[7]

"It has pleased the Eternal Architect of the world to tear from our chain of brothers one of its most deserving and beloved links. Who did not know him? Who did not esteem him? Who did not love him, our worthy Brother Mozart?

"Only a few weeks ago he stood here in our midst, glorifying with his magic sounds the dedication of our temple. Who among us would have thought then how soon he was to be taken from us? Who was to know that within three weeks we were to mourn him? It is the sad fate of men to have to leave this life with their excellent works unfinished. Kings die, leaving their incomplete plans to posterity. Artists die, after having spent their lives in perfecting their art, and general admiration follows them to the grave. Though whole nations mourn them, it is usually their fate to be forgotten by these admirers—but not by us, my brothers. Mozart's death is an irreplaceable loss to art. His talent, which already showed itself when he was a boy, made him one of the wonders of our time. Half of Europe esteemed him, the great called him their darling, and we called him—brother! Though it is proper to recall his achievements as an artist, let us not forget to honor his noble heart. He was a zealous member of our order. His love for his brothers, his cooperative and affirmative nature, his charity, his deep joy whenever he could serve one of his brethren with his special talents, these were his great qualities. He was husband and father, a friend to his friends and a brother to his brothers. He only lacked riches to make hundreds of people as happy as he would have wished them to be."

The following poem was attached to the speech:

PLATE 1.
Otto Freiherr von Gemmingen, supposedly Mozart's Masonic Godfather.

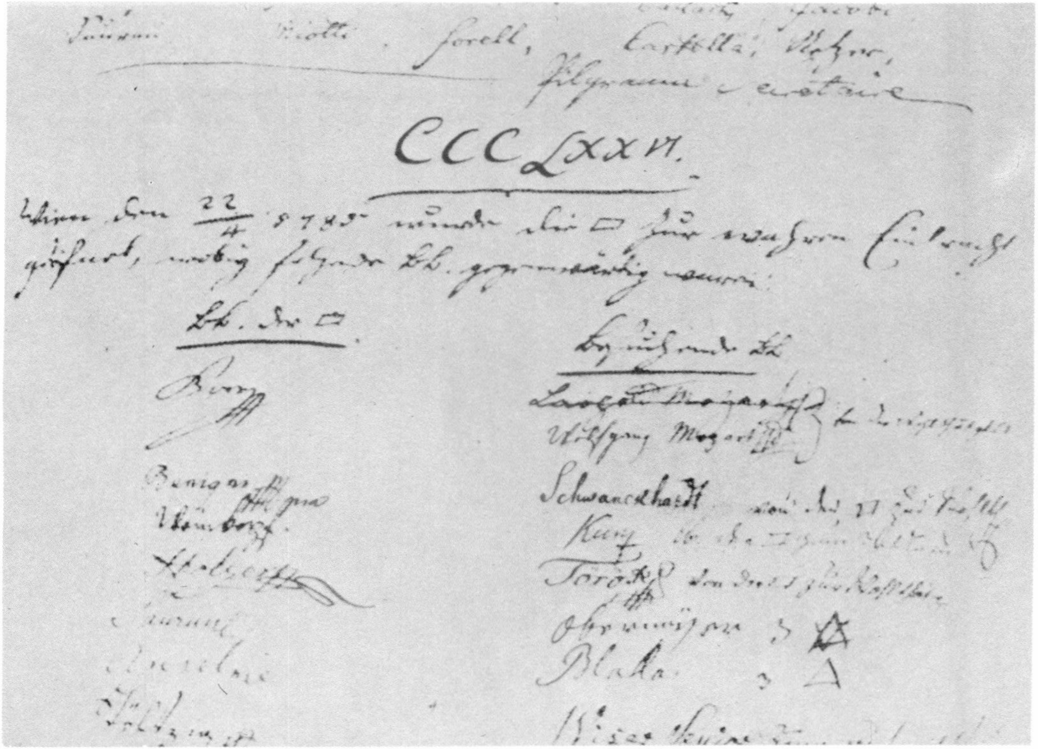

PLATE 2.

Minutes of the meeting of the "Eintracht," with the names of Leopold and W. A. Mozart.

He was in life good, mild, and gentle,
A Mason of good sense and open heart,
The muses' darling, for he re-created
In our souls what we had felt of yore.
The band is severed now, may Masons' blessing
Accompany him, bright and keen,
For our brothers' love shall also guide him
Into the land of harmony.
And we shall follow in his footsteps,
And seek out those to whom fate was unkind,
And think of him who to poor widows' dwellings
Innumerable gifts did bear.
Who built his happiness on orphans' blessings
And gave his coat to shivering poverty,
While asking only for God's reward
To be upon him in the end.
Even when lulled to sleep by Sirens' voices
Of flattery and fame, he could enjoy
The happy eyes of his poorer brethren
And never once forgot to be a man.[8]

There is no doubt that Mozart had truly accepted the Masonic view of life, especially the teachings of the third degree. This is shown in a letter, frequently quoted, which he wrote to his father on April 4, 1787, when Leopold was seriously ill:

"Death is (to be exact) the ultimate purpose of life and therefore, during the last few years, I have acquainted myself so thoroughly with this truest and best friend of man, that his image has not only ceased to frighten me, but has become a source of great comfort. And I can only thank God for having afforded me the opportunity (you will understand what I mean) to see in death the key to true happiness." Further on he writes, apparently referring to the Masonic secret, "I hope and wish that your condition is improving while I am writing these lines. If, however, contrary to all expectations, you do not feel better, then I implore you by . . . . not to make a secret of it but to tell me the truth so that I may be in your arms as soon as is humanly possible. I implore you by all that we hold sacred."

A MASONIC ALBUM FROM
MOZART'S DAY

IN THE Viennese *Nationalbibliothek* there is a manuscript album, numbered 209 979-A, entitled "Dedicated to the worthy and dear brothers and Freemasons by B. Kronauer, 5783." Masonic emblems, such as the six-cornered star, the triangle, the trowel, and the square surround the inscription on the title page. Then follow approximately 70 pages of entries by brother Masons. We know little about Brother Kronauer except that he lived in Vienna. He was born in 1743 and died March 2nd, 1799 in Vienna. His wife was Sophie (1747-1830). We do know that Kronauer had the title "von Waldeck," that he came from Winterthur, and that he was a teacher of French. He belonged to the lodge "Zur gekrönten Hoffnung."

The album contains a large number of names significant in Mozart's life. We may assume that he associated with many of the persons who wrote entries. The index at the end of the album contains 74 names, the 63rd of which is *Mozart Compositeur*. Of course this entry is of greatest interest. It begins in English:

"Patience and tranquillity of mind contribute more to cure our distempers as the whole art of medicine." (sic)

"Wien, March 30, 1787."

It continues in German: "Your sincere friend and brother Mason, Wolfgang Amadé Mozart, member of the lodge 'Zur neugekrönten Hoffnung' in the Orient of Vienna."

The most striking thing about this entry is the English quotation, written in Latin script instead of the Gothic running hand which was ordinarily used by Mozart. It is likely that he was polishing up his English at that time. He once referred to himself as an "arch-Englishman" and seems to have participated in the Anglomania then current in Vienna. This was also the time that he planned to go to England for an indeterminate period, a plan which was bitterly opposed by his father. Wolfgang had wanted to send his children to Salzburg to live with their grandfather, while Wolfgang stayed in England. But Leopold would not hear of it. At this time Mozart had a number of pupils from the British Isles, the Irish tenor Michael Kelly, the English composer Thomas Attwood and the musician Steven Storace, whose charming sister Nancy had first sung the role of Susanna in *Figaro*.

Further interesting entries in the album include no. 41, by Gemmingen: "*Naturam sequere ducem 21* Otto v. Gemmingen, $\overline{\text{III}}$ Master of the Lodge 'Zur Wohltätigkeit' in the Orient of Vienna." A silhouette of the writer is included, as is also the case with Ignaz von Born, whose intellectual face is shown on his own page. It is inscribed with a distych:

> Omne tulit punctum qui miscuit utile dulci.
> Utile qui dulci miscuit, omne tulit.
> (Signed L. [!] B.)

Speaking of Born, we should also mention the poet and writer Johann Baptist Alxinger, whose fame was great in 18th century Vienna. His entry in the album is no. 26. His role in Mozart's life is secondary and revolves around Mozart's pupil, Maria Theresia von Trattner, wife of a rich printer and paper manufacturer. Mme. von Trattner, like Frau Gottsched and Marianne Ziegler in Leipzig, was a literary bluestocking, and Alxinger satirized her. His sarcastic entry in Kronauer's album is "*Rara est concordia fratrum,*" dated Feb. 19, 5785; and with his signature, "member of the very honorable lodge St. Joseph, royal and imperial court agent." This is certainly characteristic of his satire; his words evidently refer to the scandalous quarrels among the brothers, associated with the Masonic revolution of 1785.

Another literary figure in Vienna was Alois Blumauer, whom Leopold Mozart mentions as the companion of Born on a trip to Gastein. His entry is no. 5, and he signs himself as speaker and member of the lodge "Zur wahren Eintracht" (true harmony) in Vienna, and royal imperial book censor. He quotes Horace:

> "Rebus angustis animosus atque fortis appare."

Also among the contributions of literary figures is no. 22: "Joseph Franz Ratschky, resident secretary in Linz, speaker and member of the lodge Zur wahren Eintracht." It is dated Nov. 13, just before Mozart's initiation. Ratschky is the poet of Mozart's *Gesellenreise*.

When Leopold Mozart was visiting Vienna early in 1784, the actor and dramatist Johann Heinrich Müller, alias Schröter (1738-1815) gave a banquet for 21 guests. The meal was described by Leopold in praising but not superlative terms. Müller was also associated with Wolfgang Mozart. In the *Fasching* carnival period of 1783, Mozart staged a pantomime, furnishing both choreography and music, for which Müller wrote some verses. Mozart was critical of his future brother's poems: "The verses, if we can call them that, could stand improvement. They are not my product. The actor Müller has whipped them up." Müller was from Halberstadt and had been a theologian at Halle. He had come to the Vienna *Hoftheater* in 1763, and occasionally had business with Mozart in the days of the intrigues concerning the opera *La finta semplice*. Müller's entry, no. 51, is dated Oct. 17, 1786. He identified himself as a member of "Zur wahren Eintracht" and wrote:

"The shadow on a sun dial
And a false friend
Are equal. For both can be seen
Only while the sun is shining.

May you see no cloudy weather. But if you should, I wish you friends who are visible in it. Your sincere brother and devoted servant

J. H. F. Müller, member of the royal imperial national theater."

The secretary of the above-mentioned Baron von Gemmingen was Leopold Aloys Hoffmann, originally a zealous and enlightened Mason who later turned Judas to the Craft. At this time he was professor at the University of Ofen (Budapest) and a member of the lodge "Zur Wohltätigkeit." His entry was written at the time of Mozart's initiation which, however, he did not attend. It is similar to a poem by Matthias Claudius:

"The world is a stage. You enter, look, pass, and are forgotten, no matter who you are. You are lucky if this thought does not disturb you, and it will not if wisdom and virtue live peacefully under your roof.

"8 30 4   This as a souvenir of your friend and
—
x
brother L. A. Hoffmann
Professor at Ofen in Hungary.
Member and Secretary of the
lodge 'Zur Wohltätigkeit' in Vienna."

Another interesting entry is that of the Swedish resident consul, Brother Baron Engeström, a member of the lodge "Zur gekrönten Hoffnung," dated March 9, 1784. Close to it is a verse written on July(?) 10, 1783, by the royal Swedish conductor, Kraus, a native of Mannheim:

(in French) "The things we see daily
Are not those we know best."

In the lodge meetings Mozart must have become acquainted with the musician Joseph Zistler, Master of the lodge "Zur Sicherheit" (security) in Bratislava, and a member, along with Dittersdorf, of the orchestra of the Bishop of Grosswardein. The index of the album identifies him as the Senior Warden of that lodge, and conductor to Prince Grassalkowitz. His entry was written in Bratislava on September 27, 1785. The so-called composer Bauernjöpel is also represented by a rather long poem and a silhouette.

Perhaps it would be appropriate to discuss some entries in the album written by brothers not living in Vienna. There is Brother Friedrich Münter from Copenhagen, member of the lodge "Zum Lauten-Kranz" (lute wreath) in Gotha. The Jewish locket-maker Abramson from Berlin wrote one piece in Hebrew and another in German: "Happy is he who completely knows pure sunlight." They are dated July 1, 1788. Another foreign brother is the painter H. T. Löwen from Berlin, who wrote on Sept. 26, 1784: "Be happy, love without quarreling, possess without unpleasantness. . . ." Entries in Hebrew are not rare. Brother Brabbée, royal imperial exchange commissioner and member of the "Beständigkeit" lodge, wrote with some ambiguity, "Here lies buried the dog." A member of the same lodge, Professor Michaeler, librarian of the University of Vienna, quotes Genesis 14:18 in Hebrew. Wenzel Tobias Epstein, a man formerly of Jewish faith, Second Warden and member of the lodge "Zur gekrönten Hoffnung" and a government secretary in Tyrol, wrote: "Rabbi Schamuensohn said, 'Respect your apprentices as yourself. Look up to your fellow men as if they were your teachers. Obey your masters as if they were appointed by God.' from the original text of the Mishnah Abot." Another brother of Jewish descent was the Deputy Master of the lodge "Zur Beständigkeit" and treasurer of the Austrian regional lodge. He was the physician Dr. Ehrenstein, whose entry is no. 24, dated Sept. 9, 1784, and written in Vienna:

(Latin) "Cuncta elementa gero, sum Terra, est ossibus ignis, Aether inest naribus, vulva ministrat Aquam

(French) Remember, dear and esteemed one, your faithful and sincere Brother Ehrenstein."

There are a number of other interesting entries, all relevant to a picture of Mozart's circle of Masonic friends. We can mention only a few more names: Wilkowitz (member of the "Crowned Hope" lodge and counsel of the ecclesiastic court in Linz), Brother Lang (of the same lodge, councillor to Prince Leiningen), Brother Weber (court secretary of the Netherlands office), and Professor Weissegger from Freiburg-im-Breisgau, both of the lodge "True Harmony"; Brother Laurentz Haschka of the St. Joseph lodge; Baron von Riedheim, captain in Galicia; another Brother Weber, speaker of the lodge "Zur Sicherheit" (security) in Bratislava and book dealer; and many more. A number of entries consist of cabalistic number exercises, a matter of great interest which must be discussed elsewhere.

MASONIC MUSIC BEFORE MOZART

M ost Masonic music has yet to be discovered by musicologists. Although many famous composers were members of
the Craft and composed a considerable amount of Masonic music,
the professional music historians of later times have not occupied
themselves with the subject. There are two reasons. First, older
Masonic compositions are rather rare. The original song books,
which were easily available to the layman, have been collected
by lodges and withdrawn from the public. They are difficult to
locate today even in large libraries. A more important reason is
that early Masonic music reflects the fact that it was written for
particular occasions. Only the Masonic parts of the *Magic Flute*
and the *Funeral Music* can be truly described as having general
Masonic significance. The works of lesser composers are on a much
lower artistic level and usually sound very conventional. Mozart's
supreme importance lies in the fact that, due to his particular
nature and background he was able to transmit his mystical experiences to music. One need think only of the priests' chorus,
"Oh Isis and Osiris," in the *Magic Flute,* in which an almost mysterious effect is achieved by the descending parallel sixths, reminiscent of medieval *Fauxbourdon.*
  Masonic music can be divided into three classes. The first consists of various songs and instrumental pieces which were composed
ad hoc for use at lodge meetings, dinners, the St. John's feast,
and other occasions. It is functional music. The second category
comprises music which was not originally intended for Masonic
occasions, but whose contents made it appropriate for such use.
Compositions of a moral or edifying character, such as Mozart's
cantata *Die ihr des unermesslichen Weltalls Schöpfer ehrt* (K.
619), are typical. The third and highest group includes compositions which are intended to express the Masonic creed but are
not for use in ceremonies. In addition to the *Magic Flute* and
Masonic Funeral Music, already mentioned, a composition by

29

Naumann, *Osiris,* could be classified here. In Lenning's *Handbuch der Freimaurerei* we find the following requirements for Masonic music: "Aesthetics has not yet found a formula for determining true Masonic music. One would, however, expect dignity and contentedness, and even banquet music must not become noisy." Obviously these are the minimum requirements for functional music, but Mozart's masterpieces cannot be evaluated by these standards.

Music played a more active role in 18th century Masonic life than today's. We can trace the basic shifts in Masonry through the changes in use of music. In the 18th century, since Masonry had a predominantly social character, Masonic music consisted largely of social songs. But today Masonry is primarily a spiritual matter and, accordingly, the purpose of music is to elevate and unite the spirits of the assembled. Music then assumes a religious aspect. Practically all religious communities have accepted the great unifying power of music, a power rooted in rhythm. The great force of the Roman Catholic church was partially due to the potency of its music, and Martin Luther certainly knew what he was doing when he introduced congregational singing into the reformed church.

The power of music to function as a unifying force has been demonstrated by the economist Bücher in his book *Arbeit und Rhythmus* (work and rhythm). Music with appropriate rhythmic structure not only increases the efficiency but also heightens the pleasure of working. This is achieved because musical rhythm reinforces the rhythms of the human physiology and because it decreases the controlled consciousness, introducing pleasant sensations similar to those effected by narcotics. Industrial music is based on these processes. Masons, too, use music as a source of efficiency. As the member enters the Temple, the sound of the organ lifts him out of his daily routine into a more sublime state of mind and a spiritual unity with his brothers. This effect is also produced by the uniform clothing and signs.

In order to discuss Masonic music before Mozart we must descend from these elevated thoughts into the depths of musical bibliography. It would not be possible even to mention all of the entries in this bibliography, and instead of dealing with the older Masonic music in detail here, I can only promise to do so in a future study.

Music played a prominent part in the Craft from the beginning, not only at lodge meetings but also at the dinners following them.

Thus lodges in all countries tried to attract musicians who, in turn, were glad to gain admission because of the accompanying social advantages. Shortly after the founding of the Grand Lodge of London, not later than 1725, a society, *Philo Musicae et Architecturae Societas Appolinis,* came into being and was still in existence in 1727. Only Freemasons could be invited as its guests. William Gulston was its president and Brother Francesco Xaverio Geminiani was "Director of all Musical Performances." Founded by members of the lodge "At the Queen's Head" in Hollis Street, it was to be an association of Masons interested in music. A similar one was the "Anacreontic Society," one of whose members presumably composed the famous song "Anacreon in Heaven," whose tune was later used for "The Star-Spangled Banner." Soon, however, the society *Philo Musicae,* contrary to the rules, began to admit members independently and encountered the objections of the Grand Lodge. Some documents in the library of the British Museum indicate that at this early date musicians were already uniting in the name of Masonry.

Geminiani, one of the founders of the society, was the greatest violinist of his time and a composer of considerable importance. But gradually music began to play a smaller part in the activities of the society.

Many brilliant musicians of the period were Freemasons and held offices in the lodges, for example, Charles King, organist of St. Paul's Cathedral, Master of the lodge "King's Arms" in 1725. A member of that lodge was John Immyns, who became assistant to J. C. Pepusch[1] after he was expelled from the society of attorneys, and who founded the Madrigal Society in 1741. There were other important musician Masons. John Shore, inventor of the tuning fork, was a member of the "Griffin" lodge in Newgate Street. Morris Green belonged to the lodge which met at the "Ship's Tavern." He was Sergeant Trumpeter to George III, and his successor in that office, Valentine Snow, belonged to the lodge which met at the Rainbow Coffee Tavern. Handel wrote several works for Snow, including the Trumpet Obligatos in the *Messiah, Judas Maccabeus,* and other oratorios. William Boyce was also a prominent Freemason and composed the song "No sect in the world can with Masons compare" which is still being sung today. Arne was another member of the Craft, along with Samuel Wesley, William Hayes, John Stafford Smith, Samuel Arnold, Mozart's pupil Thomas Attwood, Samuel Webbe, the composer of several Masonic choirs, and Benjamin Cook. George Smart, well known as an admirer of Beethoven, was Second Grand Organist of the Grand Lodge. Sir Michael Costa, conductor at the King's Theater, the Philharmonic Society, and the Italian Opera, was Grand Organist. This position was also held by Charles Edward Horsley, the composer of the song "Masonic Trinity." The "Entered Apprentice's Song" by Matthew Birkhead, still in use, also dates from that period. It is a typical English popular song, in the style close to British folk music.

In 1763 Thomas Hale published his *Social Harmony*, the content of which is largely Masonic, and which includes an "Ode to Freemasonry" by Brother William Hayes. A similar anthology, *Apollonian Harmony*, is "a collection of scarce and celebrated Glees, Catches, Madrigals, Canzonets, Rounds and Canons," which contains "The Free Mason's Glee" by Charles Dibdin (1745-1840), a famous actor and composer. A large number of such anthologies provided music for all kinds of Masonic social gatherings. Smollett Holden published *A Selection of Masonic Songs* (glees, duets, songs, and canons) in 1795 or 1796, in Dublin. It contains the song "To Old Hiram in Heaven where he sat in full glee," which was sung to the tune of the previously-mentioned "Anacreon in Heaven" by John Stafford Smith. All of these collections are notated in figured bass.

This type of notation is also used in a collection published at The Hague in 1766 with the title *La lire maçonne, ou Recueil de Chansons des Francs Maçons* by the Brothers de Vignoles and du Bois, with song-texts in French and Dutch. The melodies are mostly taken from French vaudeville, but there are also some original songs, designated *nouvelles compositions,* some of them by Ignatz Vitzthum. Many of the texts are set to popular tunes, dances (minuets, gavottes, bourrées) and street songs. Others again are well-known tunes from French *opéra comique.* The tune of the Masonic song *L'homme toujours s'agit pour trouver le bonheur* seems to have been taken from the aria *Dans ma cabane obscure* in Jean Jacques Rousseau's *Devin du Village. Que l'ordre qui nous enchaine* was sung to the tune of *Ton humeur, Catharine,* a street tune which was used by Italian comedians in a parody of Lully's *Armide. Chantons le bonheur des Maçons* was sung to the popular tune *Joconde,* which also appears as an aria in *Arlequin*

Atys. The tune used for *Fondement de l'art* was *Revenant de Lorette*, which also is sung by Bacchus in a parody of *Armide* to the text *Ta voix s'est fait entendre dans la Bachique Cour*.

An example of an English tune used in this collection is "God Save Great George, our King," set to a Dutch poem, *D'Ongeweinsheid*. *De Vergenoeging* is set to a German tune, *Ihr Schönen, höret an*, from the song collection, *Die singende Muse an der Pleisse* by Sperontes, a tune ascribed to J. S. Bach.

Several Masonic song books were also published in the United States. We mention only *The Masonick Minstrel*, a "selection of masonick, sentimental and humorous songs, duets, glees, canons, rounds and canzonets," printed in Dedham by H. Mann & Co., 1816. In this book there are also songs of varying origins for lodge meetings and social occasions. For the opening of the lodge, "God Save the King" became "Hail Masonry Divine." There is a canon for ten voices to honor the Grand Master, composed by Brother G. K. Jackson. Another, for singing at installations, was set to the tune of "Anacreon in Heaven," beginning with the words "When Earth's foundation first was laid." There is a "Senior Warden's Song" by T. S. Webb, to be sung first by one, then two, and finally three voices. For the St. John's festival there is an ode by Brother O. Shaw and another by Brother S. Holyoke, "Let there be light," for the consecration of a lodge. The dirge, "Solemn strikes the funeral chime," which is also used for the third degree, seems to be derived from an older source.[2]

The book contains many simple songs but also some polyphonic ones such as the "convivial Masonic canon" by Jackson, "May all the Universe be Free," set for ten voices. The collection is a hodge-podge of tunes from everywhere. For example, the glee "Hail, mysterious, glorious science" is set to Reinhard Keiser's *Auf die Gesundheit aller Mädchen* (to the good health of all girls). Mozart's *Das klinget so herrlich* (Oh listen, what is it that tinkles so clear) from the *Magic Flute* becomes a part-song, "Away with melancholy." Most of the songs have a popular character, and some are on a rather low artistic level.

The important part played by Freemasonry in English social life can be deduced from the fact that a kind of Masonic ballad-opera, *The Generous Freemason*, had been composed and performed already in 1730. It is by Brother Rufus William Chetwood, prompter at the Drury Lane Theatre from 1722 on. It was printed in

1731 by G. Roberts in Warwick Lane and contains a detailed dedication to all English dignitaries in Masonry. The plot is one of those rather sentimental stories of rescue in foreign lands, so fashionable in England at the time. An ode to Neptune by Henry Carey, part of a Neptune ballet, is one of its features. Years later, on Dec. 29, 1780, *Harlequin Freemason,* a pantomime by Dibdin, was performed at Covent Garden, produced by Messink, a friend of Garrick.

Turning now to Germany, we must first examine a work by Sperontes, *Die singende Muse an der Pleisse,* of 1736. According to Philipp Spitta, Sperontes was the pseudonym of Johann Sigismund Scholze, a Silesian; the historical significance of his collection lies in the fact that it contains a large number of hit tunes from the middle of the 18th century. It was intended to have the widest possible appeal and thus included something for all segments of society. Significantly, Scholze (who probably was a Mason) included a song for Freemasons. This song was included in a Masonic collection of 1745, one year before the first official Masonic song book made its appearance *(Freymäurer Lieder* by Ludwig Friedrich Lenz). The song itself mentions "our Order," complaining that it is much misunderstood. Printed under the title are the Masonic emblems, square, plumb rule, and compass. There is so little secrecy about these Masonic matters that Masonic songs could be included in a general song collection in the same way as students' and soldiers' songs, so little secrecy, indeed, that a noble lady from Thuringia was able to include French Masonic songs in a manuscript collection made for her own amusement. In the *Singende Muse* the so-called French method of parody is used; new words are sung to the tunes of songs already well-known. The French Masonic collections employed the same process.

We now should examine some of the best-known German Masonic collections. Like the French and Dutch ones, they are closely linked to contemporary native song writing. The first one was set down in Altenburg and published in 1746, but the music of its nine songs is uninteresting. In 1749 appeared the first collection by a German musician, Johann Adolf Scheibe (1708-1776), whose name is important in the history of Masonic music, and who also acquired fame of another sort because of his opposition to J. S. Bach. When the organist of the St. Thomas church in Leipzig, Christian Gräbner, died in 1729, several musicians, among them Scheibe, applied for the position. Scheibe was unsuccessful and the post went to Görner. Bach was cantor of the church at the time, and a member of the committee which judged the candidates. Scheibe later moved to Hamburg where he edited a periodical, *Critischer Musicus,* in whose sixth issue he attacked Bach violently, calling his music "as tortuous as it is futile because it is contrary to all reason." Bach replied by composing one of his most beautiful secular cantatas, *The Contest between Phoebus and Pan.* In this cantata he mocked Scheibe, representing him by the character of Midas, much as Wagner satirized the critic Eduard Hanslick, who had attacked him, in the figure of Beckmesser in *Die Meistersinger.*

It is to Brother Scheibe's great credit that he did his best to rectify his error some years later. The following passage appeared in *Critischer Musicus* on July 28, 1739:

"Some time ago in a famous city there lived a person whom I can describe very accurately because I have been close to him since childhood and know him as well as myself. Let us call him Alfonso. Circumstances forced him to make his living by music. As he made progress, he began to feel envious of the advantages of others. And when he heard the ability of experienced men praised, he would envy them simply because he did not possess the same skill. Later this envy, which had held him captive, changed to ambition, which spurred him on to the emulation of famous men. Thus he gradually overcame his weakness and was able to hear others praised without blushing. Finally, he became able to extol them himself and to acknowledge their right to fame."

This act was truly in the Masonic spirit. Scheibe was one of the most formidable theorists and critics of his day. One of his lasting claims to fame is his theory that polyphonic music originated in the North of Europe, an opinion that has never been discarded. Scheibe was less important as a musician, however, and Masonic music would be richer today if his adversary Bach had entered the Craft.

Scheibe's competitor for the post of organist at the St. Thomas church, Görner, who was the cause of this quarrel with Bach, had a brother who also influenced Masonic music. In his "Collection of New Odes and Songs" (1742), all of the song-texts were written by Friedrich von Hagedorn and set to music in the manner of

French vaudeville. This collection is distinguished by popular, vulgar melodies resembling dance tunes. Görner was responsible, however, for at least one innovation; he was the first to commit to paper a practice which had probably been in use for some time. He introduced antiphonal or responsorial singing into some of the brief songs intended for small, friendly gatherings. Some especially short songs, and others with little musical interest can be improved if the refrain or even the body of the song is sung alternately by two groups or by a leader and a chorus.

Freemasons, not students, were thus the first to use antiphonal singing in German art song. In the first collection mentioned above, published in 1746, there are no antiphonal songs, but the second one, *Neue Freimäurer Lieder,* dedicated to the lodge "Zorobabel" in Copenhagen, and dated St. John's day, 5749, already has some. "Now sings one, now sing all," it declares in the preface. The arrangement of the verses in most of the songs shows quite clearly how this is to be done. The music, by Scheibe, is rather insipid. In 1776, the year of his death, Scheibe published a "Complete Songbook for Freemasons in two Volumes" *(Vollständiges Liederbuch für Freymäurer mit Melodien in zwei Büchern).* The chorus had by then become polyphonic, but it is arranged in such a way that musically untrained brothers could also sing it. The second volume of this work was published by Christian Gottlob Proft in Copenhagen in 1785, but it is not mentioned in the bibliography of Eitner, or in the works of Kretzschmar and Friedländer. People seem to have been aware of Scheibe's weakness as a composer, for this new collection, with compositions by other brothers, was published rather hurriedly. In its preface it mentioned thirteen Masonic song books on which it has drawn for material, thereby enriching our bibliographical knowledge. A large number of the songs are by a new composer, J. Gottl. Naumann. The songs are placed in order according to Masonic categories:

> Opening of the lodge
> St. John's festival
> Toast to the King
> Toast to the Protector
> Master Masons' songs
> Fellow Crafts' songs
> Entered Apprentices' songs

Encouragements
Wisdom
Beauty
Strength
Liberty
Secrecy
Unity
Holy Number
Joy
The ladies
Music
Song to peace
The poor
Closing songs

The songs are scored for clavier accompaniment as were all songs of that time. They are designed to be "sung at the clavier." But the score contains only the vocal melody and a figured bass, rather than a full clavier part like that of the classical composers.

Some songs in the collection have been taken from Roman Catholic hymnody. For example, *Lasst uns singen des Weisen Ruh* (let us sing to the wise man's peace), which was included in the "wisdom" group, appears to be based on the hymn *Grosser Gott, wir loben Dich* (Great God, we praise Thee), according to Bäumker *(Das katholische deutsche Kirchenlied* IV, p. 285). This tune was widespread throughout the later eighteenth century, having already appeared in the hymnal of Empress Maria Theresia (published in 1774).

Naumann's song of strength ("The faith that binds us brothers is more durable than steel") is vaguely similar to Papageno's aria " 'Tis love, they say, love only" from the *Magic Flute,* and possibly it served as a model for Mozart. Very numerous in the collection are the table songs which, understandably, are largely patterned after students' songs. The various toasts to lords, ladies, and artists, which are today spoken, were then expressed in musical form.

Beethoven's teacher, Christian Gottlob Neefe (1748-1798), also seems to have been a Freemason, Wolfstieg and Irmgard Leux notwithstanding. In a collection of songs, *Freimaurerlieder zum Gebrauche der ger. und vollk. Loge zum* (!) *drey H*(ammern

37

in Naumburg) *aufgesetzt von E*(rnst) *Johann Georg S*(chmidt?), *hrsg. von F*(riedrich) *Gotthilf F*(reitag?) *(Mit Melodien von Fenee) Leipzig, Breitkopf 1774.* The name of the composer is given as Fenee, for the inversion of Neefe into Fenee was common Masonic practice. Perhaps Beethoven's interest in Freemasonry was due to his teacher's influence. According to recent research, Neefe was a member of the lodge "Karoline zu den drei Pfauen" (Caroline of the three peacocks), and in 1784, also prefect of the Bonn chapter of the Illuminati, under the name of Glaucus. The six songs in the Neefe collection are to be sung in "assembly," i.e., in a closed lodge meeting. Four years later yet another collection was published for use at lodge meetings (published by Bock, Hamburg), established by the German Grand Lodge. The next year, a second volume appeared, published, according to Friedländer, by C. G. Telonius.

We have already mentioned Joh. G. Naumann (1741-1801), conductor at the court chapel in Dresden, as one of the most remarkable Mason musicians of his time. He seems to have been very highly esteemed in Masonic circles, for he was granted admission into a very exclusive lodge in Dresden whose members prided themselves on their aristocratic origin. His collection, which was published in Berlin in 1782 with the title *40 Freimaurer Lieder,* was intended for use at the dinners of German and French lodges. It is dedicated to Prince Frederick William of Prussia. A large number of the songs are identical with those of the Copenhagen collection mentioned above. Naumann was quite an able and industrious composer, but not one of genius. His songs tend to sound tearfully sentimental, and the Masonic ones are no exception. The collection also contains some short instrumental compositions which were probably used as ritual music. A piece to be played on entering the lodge is in the form of a simple song with three recurring beats representing the Entered Apprentice's knocking. The three-fold handshake, with which the chain is broken, is represented by three dotted notes at the end. The idea of the chain is doubtlessly expressed in a piece characterized by chains of suspensions.

After the publication of his song collection, Naumann wrote an opera, *Osiris.* His chief biographer, Richard Engländer, says that Naumann probably felt the need of stating his Masonic creed in a piece of large proportions. We shall return to this opera, first produced in Dresden in 1781, which anticipated the *Magic Flute* by ten years in its use of Masonic lore as the main theme. According to Engländer, *Osiris* was one of the few operas of the time whose dramatic content fully satisfied the standards of Gluck and Calzabigi.

At the time Naumann was engaged in composing this opera, Lorenzo DaPonte, Mozart's librettist, was in Dresden staying with Mazzolà, who wrote the text of *Osiris*. Since DaPonte was helping Mazzolà in his general dramatic work, it is quite probable that he also had a hand in the creation of *Osiris*. Mazzolà later revised Metastasio's libretto *Titus* for Mozart's opera, *La Clemenza di Tito,* which was performed in Prague in 1791 for the coronation of Emperor Leopold II as King of Bohemia. We do not know whether Mozart or Schikaneder heard about *Osiris* from DaPonte, or even from Mazzolà himself, but we can safely look upon it as a forerunner of the *Magic Flute.* This is evident in the tests which are reminiscent of Masonic ritual, opposition of good and evil, the priests' choruses, etc. Furthermore, Naumann uses a kind of *Leitmotif*-technique which seems to confirm his position as a transition between the late Neapolitan composers and the romantic opera. The most important Masonic characteristic of *Osiris* is the repeated appearance of a series of beats which function as rhythmic *Leitmotifs.*

We should also mention a volume containing Masonic songs by Carl Friedrich Ebers (1770-1836), a composer from Mecklenburg. It is inscribed, "15 Masonic Songs for all occasions at the Festive Board, performed at the united lodges in the Orient of Berlin, set to music and respectfully dedicated to the *National-Mutterloge zu den drei Weltkugeln* (the national mother-lodge 'Three Globes'), to the *Grosse Landesloge von Deutschland* (grand lodge of Germany), and to the Grand Lodge 'Royal York zur Freundschaft' by Carl Friedrich Ebers, member of the lodge *Zum flammenden Stern* (flaming star)" (published by Fröhlich & Co.). The subjects of the songs are the king, the Master of the lodge, the lodge and its officers, members of the Craft, new initiates, the charity box, the ladies, St. John's festival, etc. Like Naumann, Ebers uses Masonic rhythms. For example, in the song *Der Hammer,* the rhythm of the Entered Apprentice's knocks can be heard in the piano introduction. Both the music and the words are inept, although some of the poets, such as Anschütz, an actor and member of the lodge "Apollo" in Leipzig, Diemer, Kern-dorfer, and Eberhard are quite well-known. The only non-Masonic song composed by Ebers is the German popular tune *Wir sind drei Könige der Welt* (Böhme, *Volkstümliche Lieder der Deutschen,* p. 421). Ebers appears in a dissertation, *Die Mecklen-burger Liederkomponisten des 18. Jahrhunderts* by Hans Rentzow, but his Masonic activities and compositions are not mentioned there.

A large number of musical works composed for specific Masonic occasions were published in England and France as well as Germany and Austria. An interesting example is a work entitled *Apologie pour l'Ordre des Francs-Maçons par Mr. N[audot], Membre de l'Ordre, Avec deux Chansons, composée par le Frère Américain.* This is doubtless a vaudeville song adapted for Masonic uses. To my essay, "Old Freemason Music" in *Musical Quarterly,* the editor added the note: "It has been asserted that this Brother was none other than Benjamin Franklin."

I should like to add a few words about Masonic music in France, which has been discussed in an excellent article by Roger Cotte in *Die Musik in Geschichte und Gegenwart.* According to Cotte, music was frequently performed in the earliest French lodges, beginning in 1725. As in the *Lire Maçonne,* the songs consist largely of *vaudevilles* and *pontneufs,* but there were also some which had been especially composed for the occasion. One of the most important collections was made by one Jean Jacques Naudot, presumably the famous flutist who lived in Paris between 1726 and 1745. The manuscript of this collection has been pre-served by the Paris Conservatoire and has the title (in French), "Notated songs of the very worshipful brotherhood of Free-masons, preceded by several pieces of poetry on the same subject, and a march." It was translated into German several times. The collection contains several original compositions, a male chorus for three voices (even here the symbolic number three!), and two marches for several instruments. One of the latter was transcribed for clavecin by Michel Corrette, and the flutist Blavet arranged the *Marche de la grande Loge de la Maçonnerie* for two flutes.

As in Anglo-Saxon Masonry, great importance was attached to the marches played at French lodge meetings. Henri-Joseph Taskin (1779-1852) composed several marches as well as other Masonic music. In France, as in Austria, it was customary to perform cantatas at consecration ceremonies, and Louis Nicola Clerambault (1676-1749) composed such a work, *Les Francsmaçons*, in 1743. While he was certainly a member of the Craft, there is some doubt about the membership of Jean Philippe Rameau (1683-1764), France's foremost composer of the 18th century. We know, however, that several of his operas, including *Zoroastre*, are based on Masonic ideas.

The *Concerts de la Loge Olympique* were founded by Masonry. These concerts were started in 1780 and open only to Masons. Performances took place within the framework of a Masonic ritual. The members of the orchestra appeared in embroidered suits with lace cuffs and wore ceremonial swords and cocked hats. Queen Marie-Antoinette patronized these concerts, whose moving spirit was the famous violinist Jean Battiste Viotti (1753-1824). Luigi Cherubini had his well-known cantata *Amphyon* performed there, and Haydn contributed six of his best symphonies.

In 1801 a bowdlerized version of the *Magic Flute* was performed in Paris with the title *Les mystères d'Isis*. Its perpetrator, a Czech by the name of Wentzel Ludwig Lachnit, managed to strip the opera of all its wonderful and amusing elements. Papageno was turned into a shepherd named Bochoris, the Champagne Aria from *Don Giovanni* and an aria from *La Clemenza di Tito* were smuggled in as duets. Cotte observes that this opera had some influence on French Masonic composers, especially on Taskin.

Among other French composers who were Freemasons but did not compose any Masonic music were Boieldieu, Pleyel, and Meyerbeer, and from a later period, Henri Casadesus, Jean Armand Petit, and Prudent Pruvost. One of the best-known French Masonic songs, *Chant des Maillets,* is persistently but wrongly ascribed to Mozart, just as *Freut euch des Lebens* was always claimed for him in the England and America of 1800.

MASONIC MUSICIANS AROUND MOZART

The FIELD OF MUSIC contributed an exceptionally large number of Freemasons in the 18th century. In Germany and Austria they were especially welcomed into the lodges because their participation helped to create the solemn atmosphere necessary for the ceremonies, whose emphasis of aesthetic experience has always been primary.

We shall mention a few musicians who were members of the Austrian lodges at that time, without arranging them in any order of merit. There was Franz Zöhrer, born in Zwettl in 1749, conductor to Count Palm in Regensburg and a member of the lodge "Zu den drei Adlern" (three eagles) in Vienna. Nothing further is known about him. Another member of this lodge was Carlo d'Ordonez, a musician who, according to Abafi, was born in Vienna in 1734. Hanslick, in his *Geschichte des Concertwesens*, says that he was born in Spain, and that around 1760 he became registrar and later a secretary of the *Landgericht*. He was a proficient violinist and also composed symphonies and cantatas which were occasionally performed at the academies of the *Tonkünstlersocietät*. Both Hanslick and Abafi state that he was admitted as a member of the Imperial Court Chapel in Vienna in 1766, but his name does not appear in the register. Some chamber music and a Singspiel (musical comedy) have been preserved. He held the office of First Steward in the Scottish Rite Lodge.

Paul Wranitzky was a member of the lodge "Zur gekrönten Hoffnung." He was a violinist in Count Johann Esterhazy's private orchestra, and from 1785 until his death in 1808 he was director of the orchestra at the Vienna Court Opera. He played a part in the history of the *Magic Flute* and composed several Masonic songs.

The "Crowned Hope" lodge could also count among its members the musicians Joseph Bartha, Vittorio Colombazzo (otherwise unknown), the actor and singer Valentin Adamberger, who performed Mozart's Masonic songs; the poet-laureate of the lodge, Franz Petran, a secular priest from Bohemia who wrote the words of Mozart's cantata *Maurerfreude* (Mason's joy, K. 471); Ferdinand Schleiss (otherwise unknown), and the ballet master Carl Prandstetter. The lodge's St. John's festival of 1785 was embellished by three songs with music by Wranitzky and words by Petran.

One of Mozart's enemies was also a member of the Craft. He was Leopold Kozeluch, music teacher of the Archduchess Elisabeth, the wife of Emperor Francis II, and, after 1792, court conductor and composer to the Emperor. Kozeluch was a member of the lodge "Zum Palmbaum" (palm tree) and later of "Zu den drei Adlern" (three eagles). He had at one time tried to stir up Haydn against Mozart, and his hateful remarks at the premiere of *La Clemenza di Tito* in Prague made him unpopular with his Bohemian compatriots. Even Beethoven did not escape his venomous opposition.

Another interesting member of the "Palmbaum" lodge was Carl Leopold Röllig, an official of the court library and an excellent glass-harmonica player. He was cured of a serious illness by Cagliostro and otherwise became entangled in mystical affairs. G. A. Meissner reports that Röllig was on terms of intimate friendship with Johann Gottlieb Naumann.

Johann Holzer, member of the lodge "Zur wahren Eintracht," wrote a number of songs and Masonic compositions. Some of the songs with piano accompaniment were published in 1779, and some of these, in turn, appeared under the editorship of Irene Schlaffenberg in volume 54 of *Denkmäler der Tonkunst in Oesterreich*. Very little is known about Holzer's life. In addition to twelve German songs, he left some chamber music works, now in the archive of the *Gesellschaft der Musikfreunde* in Vienna. Anton Johann Holzer was employed at the Austrian war office. His colleague there, Joseph von Holzmeister, an amateur musician, delivered the address to the new initiates at Haydn's initiation. The speech was reproduced in the *Journal für Freymäurer*.[1] In the first volume of this periodical, 1784, two of Holzer's songs were printed. One, *Im Namen der Armen* (in the name of the poor), with words by Gottlieb Leon, beginning "Brothers, listen to the cries of the poor," is scored for two voices and cembalo accompaniment. The music is gentle and slightly reminiscent of Mozart's songs, though less formidable. The other song by Holzer is a setting of Ratschky's *Gesellenreise* (Fellow Craft's journey), published in 1785, which was also set to music by Mozart. Likewise for two voices and cembalo, it is designated as a march. Evidently it was actually performed at a ceremony.

One of the less praiseworthy Masonic compositions of Mozart's time was a circus-like pantomime, *Adoniram's Tod,* composed and conducted by one Brother Hyam, and performed by a company of dressage riders in April, 1784. A survival of the equestrian ballets of the 17th century, this "horse opera" does not contribute to the dignity of Masonic intellectual history.

A collection of Masonic songs from this period includes compositions by Brother Bauernjöpel. Its title was *Lieder zum Gebrauch der Freimaurerloge 'Zur wahren Eintracht' in W., in Musik gesetzt von Br. B-j-.* The composer was speaker of the lodge "Zur Beständigkeit" (constancy) in Vienna, and it was said that he could say "a hundred stupid things a minute with a wise face." This collection also contains a poem by Blumauer set to music by Sarti, whose Masonic status, however, is uncertain.

Three more songs from this period were performed on July 24, 1785, at the St. John's festival of the lodge "Zu den drei Feuern" (three fires) in Vienna. The first of them is intended to be sung before dinner, giving thanks for the "gifts of Mother Earth." The second is entitled "For the collection for the poor," and the third is for the closing of the lodge ("Our chain is the image of true, warm harmony"). The composer of these songs was Georg Benda, a member of the lodge in Altenburg, but at that time a resident of Vienna. The three songs are entitled "The St. John's festival of the lodge 'Three Fires' in Vienna, celebrated on July 24, 1785, set to music by Brother B-a." Mozart and Benda certainly were well acquainted even though the friendship is not documented, and Mozart was deeply impressed by Benda's *Medea* and *Ariadne auf Naxos*. Indeed, Mozart even sketched a setting of Gemmingen's *Semiramis* in the style of Benda's melodramas (plays with music background). On Nov. 12, 1778, Mozart wrote to his father: "You know that Benda has always been my favorite among the Lutheran conductors, and I am so fond of these two works that I carry them around with me."

Now a few words about the musicians in the lodges in Prague which Mozart visited. Franz Xaver Hloschek and his son Anton

44

were the only musicians in the lodge "Zu den drei gekrönten Säulen" (three crowned pillars). Their name is spelled "Loschek" in the *Jahrbuch der Tonkunst von Wien und Prag, 1796.* A member of their lodge was the physician de Vignet who not only loved music but was also a generous friend to Mozart. On June 13, 1792, he arranged a memorial concert for the benefit of Mozart's widow, in which his daughter and Mme. Duschek participated.

In addition, we should mention the following Masonic musicians and artists belonging to Lodges with which Mozart had friendly relations. The musician Schmidt(?) from Brünn belonged to the St. Joseph Lodge of which Wenzel Himmelbauer, "traveling musician," was a member. The latter was born in Bohemia, an excellent cellist who, together with Dittersdorf, was a member of the orchestra of Count Grassalkowitz. Ch. F. Schubart is quite enthusiastic about Himmelbauer's playing and his pleasant personality. According to Eitner, he supposedly lived in Bern, Switzerland. Peter Graf, another "Tonkünstler," belonged to the same Lodge. Johann Friedel, an actor of Schikaneder's theater, and the actor Karl L. Schmidt were members of the "Beständigkeit," of which also Joseph Grassi, later Professor at the *Kunstakademie* in Dresden, was a member. It was this Grassi who participated in a pantomime in February, 1783, choreographed by Mozart himself (Schenk, page 579).

MOZART'S MASONIC COMPOSITIONS

ON MARCH 26, 1785, Mozart composed his *Gesellenreise* (Fellow Craft's Journey). It is known that Leopold Mozart was passed to the second degree on April 16 of that year. Therefore it is highly probable that Wolfgang composed the song for that occasion, especially since he did not visit the lodge "Zur wahren Eintracht" between these two dates, and since prominent Masons were usually initiated there. As already indicated, Ratschky's poem was also set to music by Holzer. It is remarkable that Holzer's setting was published in the *Journal für Freymäurer* early in 1785, at about the time that Mozart was composing his setting. Holzer's choice of harpsichord for accompaniment, and Mozart's of organ, indicate the contrasting characters of these two compositions. While Holzer's rhythm and tempo are suitable for the ritual, which gives him no cause for special sentiment but is simply one step on the Mason's road, Mozart's song is gentler, and more solemn, perhaps a representation of homage to his old father. Joseph Franz von Ratschky (1757-1810), the poet, was one of the most famous writers of his day and a high-ranking civil servant. Sonnenfels had recommended him to Emperor Joseph and he ended his career as a *Staatsrat*. In 1785 he wrote an essay on "The tolerance publicly granted to the order of Freemasons by Emperor Joseph II," and in the same year his poems were published by Brother Rudolf Gräffer, in the first book printed on vellum in Vienna. Many brothers subscribed to it. It contains the poem *Gesellenreise,* which was later parodied as "Life's Journey" by D. Jäger. Ratschky had a good sense of humor.

A second song, with a poem by Brother Schittlersberg, was also set to music by Mozart (K. 483) and was designated to be performed at the opening of the lodge "Zur neugekrönten Hoffnung." Schittlersberg was Senior Warden at the lodge "Zur wahren Eintracht." The translation of the first stanza follows:

Oh sing today, beloved brothers
Your song of jubilation,
For Joseph's benevolence
Has crowned anew our hope
And in our hearts a threefold flame now gleams.

In order to understand these words, one must realize that while Joseph gave the Freemasons permission to meet, he decreased the number of lodges in Vienna from eight to three. Thus the lodges "Crowned Hope," "Charity," "St. Joseph," and "Three Fires" were dissolved, and most of their members joined the "Newly Crowned Hope." The words of the song play on the names of these lodges and otherwise refer to the merger. Since the event took place in December, 1785, we can assume that this is the time of the song's composition. It is scored for a solo voice, a three-part chorus, and organ accompaniment, and its beginning is slightly similar to the song of the three genii in the finale no. 21 of the *Magic Flute* ("The rosy flush that greets us yonder").

We see that Mozart was already beginning to use the ritual number three in the manner typical of the *Magic Flute*. A hymn for the closing of the lodge, also dating from 1785, is K. 484, for three male voices. A translation of the text as it appears in the autograph follows.

1. *Solo*   Oh you, our new leaders,
We thank you now for all your faith.
Oh lead us ever in the paths of virtue
That all rejoice in the chain that ties us,
The chain that binds us to better men,
And giveth sweetness to life's chalice,
Gives sweetness to the cup of life.

   Chorus   The holy adjuration we also vow:
To strive for perfection of our great temple.

2. *Solo*   And on the rungs of truth
Let us approach the throne of wisdom
That we may reach its holiness
And that we of her crown may be worthy,
If charity will drive out
The jealousy of the profane.

The words of this hymn indicate that it was intended for the installation of a new set of officers. Evidently both of these songs were composed for the same evening. Their words were printed with the following remark: "For the first solemn opening of the very worshipful lodge 'Newly Crowned Hope,' on the 14th of the first month, 5785." Otto Erich Deutsch has proved that this is a misprint; since the merging of the lodges took place only at the end of 1785, the date should have been 5786.

Deutsch includes the texts of two more songs, *Zur Eröffnung der Meisterloge* (for the opening of "Newly Crowned Hope") and *Zum Schluss der Meisterarbeit,* "by a brother of the lodge (i.e., Gottlieb Leon), set to music by Br. M . . ." (evidently Mozart, probably in 1786). Thus these two songs, entitled *Des Todes Werk* (the work of death) and *Vollbracht ist die Arbeit der Meister* (the work of the Masters is finished) might be two lost compositions of Mozart's. The occasion of their composition is uncertain. I suspect that they were performed at the memorial meeting of November 17 for the Duke of Mecklenburg and Count Esterhazy, at which the *Masonic Funeral Music* was also performed. The two songs are accompanied by figured bass, whose chords must be completed by the organist. This is true of another Masonic song, K. 148, written, according to Köchel, in 1772, although J. E. Engl dates it from 1784, a time when Mozart was already a Mason. The words have a Masonic ring:

> Most holy tie of brotherhood's deep friendship,
> Which equals the joy found in paradise.
> A true believer, yet not opposed
> To this world. This truth is comprehended,
> Yet kept secret.

The style and flavor of this song are very similar to those of *Gesellenreise,* and point to the "Crowned Hope" lodge. Einstein, like Köchel, accepts circumstantial evidence for the belief that Mozart wrote this song about 1772, that is, in his Salzburg period. His reasoning is that Mozart wrote no figured-bass songs after 1784, except for a parody, *Die Alte* (the old woman, K. 517). On the other hand, Wyzewa, St. Foix, and Abert are convinced that the song was composed after Mozart's initiation.

We counter Einstein's argument by asserting that two later

songs, K. 483 and 484, are also written for figured bass. But if the song was indeed composed in 1772, it would simply mean that young Mozart was already well acquainted with Masonry at the time. He also composed two German religious songs, *O Gottes Lamm* (O lamb of God) and *Als aus Aegypten Israel* (When Israel out of Egypt), K. 343, for solo voice and bass accompaniment. According to Jahn, these are really studies for Masonic music, but Einstein thinks they were written for a hymnal which Archbishop Colloredo was planning in 1782. These hymns had already been composed by 1779.

On April 20, 1785, Mozart composed the cantata *Maurerfreude* (Mason's joy). The words were written by Brother Petran for a meeting of the lodge "Zur gekrönten Hoffnung," called because Ignaz von Born had just been honored by Emperor Joseph for his latest metallurgical discovery. The secretary of the lodge, G. D. Bartsch, sent out a newsletter saying that the lodge had decided to meet and celebrate with Born, and to show him love and respect. The letter goes on to say: "Several songs were performed on this occasion, and also a cantata written by Brother Petran and set to music by our famous Brother Mozart of the very worshipful lodge 'Zur Wohltätigkeit.' It was sung by Brother Adamberger and has now been published by Brother Artaria, together with a drawing by Brother Unterberger and a preface by Brother Epstein. All profits from the sale of this work will be given to the poor, and we hope that you will do all you can to promote its sale in your neighborhood."

At this meeting the compositions of other brothers were also performed. One of them, *Bei der Almosensammlung* (collection for alms), beginning "Worthy Masons, true brethren, now it is time to think of the poor," had words by Matolay, music by Wranitzky, both members of the "Crowned Hope" lodge. It was sung by Adamberger, and the score was later published, with an engraving by Mansfeld, and sold for the benefit of the poor. Alfred Meissner, whose *Rococobilder* (Rococo sketches) is supposedly based on a diary of his grandfather's, A. G. Meissner, a member of the lodge "Zur Wahrheit und Einigkeit" (truth and unity) in Prague, says that this cantata was performed in Prague on the occasion of a visit by Mozart. As we have already said, *Maurerfreude* was first performed on April 20, 1785, in the presence of Leopold Mozart.

49

Since 1782, the "Crowned Hope" lodge had been meeting on the first floor of the house of Baron Moser (rebuilt in 1835), where a Temple had been installed. But after-meeting dinners were usually given at the "Freemason casino" Cafe Jüngling, in the Leopoldstadt district of Vienna, then Untere Donaustrasse 5, now Praterstrasse 6. The original owner, Joseph Mayer, was a member of the lodge "St. Joseph" and his successor, Johann Jüngling, belonged to the "Newly Crowned Hope," though at first as a serving brother.

The score of the cantata, with piano accompaniment, was engraved and published with a frontispiece depicting the Temple of Humanity standing in a classical landscape. The title of the cantata appears as an inscription on the temple, on whose right are two female figures as well as Ignaz von Born, in whose honor the cantata had been composed. Born stands with his right hand on his breast and is represented as an elderly bearded man. One of the female figures is putting a wreath on his head, while the other, wearing a crown, holds his hand. The inscription reads: *"Die Maurerfreude,* a cantata sung on April 24, 1785, in honor of our very worthy brother B. by the brethren of the lodge, G. H. in the O. of Vienna, words by Brother P., music by Brother W. A. Mozart; published for the benefit of the poor; available in Vienna and in the best art and book stores in Germany."

Ignaz von Born was born in Karlsburg in 1742 and died in Vienna on July 24, 1791. Originally a Jesuit, he left the order after 16 months to study law at the University of Prague. After a tour of Europe he returned to Prague, devoting all his energies to the study of natural science and founding a "Society for the Study of Mathematics, National History, and Natural History." In 1776, Empress Maria Theresia called him to Vienna to take charge of the Imperial Natural History Collection. Because of his high moral principles, his wit, and his charm, he soon became the friend of all Viennese scholars, who gathered about him in the lodge "Zur wahren Eintracht." The one-time Jesuit became one of the most outspoken opponents of monastic orders, attacking them in his famous *Monachologia.* In 1784, he wrote a detailed article on the mysteries of the Egyptians in the *Journal für Frey-mäurer.* This, coupled with his unchallenged authority on all ethical and Masonic matters, made him into an almost legendary figure. Rightly or wrongly, it has been assumed that he was the model for the character of Sarastro in the *Magic Flute*, but he did not live to see that opera performed.

The work that led the Emperor to honor Born on the occasion mentioned above was published by Brother Christian Friedrich Wappler and was entitled *Ueber das Anquicken der gold- und silberhältigen Erze, Rohsteine, Schwarzkupfer und Hüttenspeise.* It described an improved method of gold and silver mining which was introduced in all state mines by imperial decree. On this occasion the Emperor received Born and highly praised his work. Franz Gräffer, in his *Wiener Memoiren und Dosenstücke*, describes a conversation between Born and the Emperor: "This is one of the most important discoveries of the century," says the Emperor. "I could do no better than to introduce this method immediately. It is already being used in Saxony and Sweden. And here is a letter which says that they are using it even in Mexico." He hands Born a letter, enclosed in a communication sent to the Emperor by Benjamin Franklin, and Born blushes with joy. Franklin, after all, was one of the most prominent Masons in North America as well as a great scientist.

Let us return to the composition. Brother Petran, the poet, was priest to Count Thun. The tenor Adamberger, who sang the cantata at the first performance, was the father of the famous actress Toni Adamberger who later became the bride of Theodor Körner. The drawing for the beautiful engraving, by Sebastian Mansfeld, came from Ignaz Unterberger, and the work was printed by Pasquale Artaria. All these men belonged to the lodge "Zur gekrönten Hoffnung," as did Wenzel Tobias Epstein, who wrote the preface. Of Jewish descent, Epstein (1758-1824) was renowned for his chess-playing and coin-collecting, and was eventually ennobled and took the title von Ankersberg.

Ignaz von Born rigidly adhered to his Masonic convictions. In 1785, when the elector of Bavaria, Carl Theodor, decreed that all civil servants and members of the Academy of Sciences must leave the Craft, Born immediately returned all his Bavarian diplomas. He declared that he was not only unrepentant but also proud to be a Mason. He asserted that members of the Craft were distinguished by being just, obedient to God, loyal to their country, and charitable to their fellow-men. In spite of all this he later renounced Masonry, for reasons unknown, and resigned from the lodge. On

April 27, 1787, he wrote the following in Mozart's album, in Latin:

"Sweet Apollo, who hast given thy art, thy gifts to our Mozart so that he may provide sounds with his strings to him who demands them, sounds which my hand also desires, sharp, deep, quick, slow, harmonious, plaintive, loud, soft sounds, blending without offense, bring it about that his pleasing lyre may sound with his music for many happy days, and grant the harmony of a pleasant fate."

In the library of the Munich conservatory there is a manuscript score of the cantata *Maurerfreude,* with an ecclesiastic text superimposed. The music has been arranged for soprano, tenor, alto, bass, trumpets, and drums. Possibly this Masonic composition was used to fight Masonic ideas after the collapse of the movement in Bavaria, for the new words begin: "See how the power of this heresy is disappearing." Mozart composed the cantata especially for Brother Adamberger, taking care to accommodate his vocal and artistic qualities. Therefore, the main portion is a long tenor solo, the beginning of which is in the style of an Italian concert aria. Then follows a recitative beginning, "See how wisdom and virtue turn with favor to the son of Masons," and an accompanied andante recitative: "Take, beloved, this crown from the hands of our eldest son, from Joseph. This is the greatest joy of Masons, yes, this is the triumph of Masonry." At the word "Joseph" the tempo suddenly quickens to express the jubilant moment. Again the dotted eights present Masonic rhythms. The allegro movement which follows is for tenor solo, two tenors, and bass. It can be performed by a chorus or soloists but, if we consider the small number of lodge members, and especially the few good voices, the possibility of a performance by only three singers is very great.

The second among the larger Masonic works is the *Kleine Freimaurerkantate* (little Masonic cantata) K. 623, with words by Emanuel Schikaneder, written for the consecration of the temple of the lodge "Zur neugekrönten Hoffnung" during November, 1791. As we shall see, Schikaneder was not a member of that lodge, and it is not quite clear how he came to write the words. We may assume that Mozart, with whom he was working on the *Magic Flute,* had been asked to furnish the cantata. In any case, Lewis is mistaken in naming Schikaneder among the outstanding members of this lodge. The cantata is the last work completed by

Mozart and also the last entry in his own handwritten list of compositions. It was published in 1792 by Joseph Hraschansky, a former member of the "True Harmony" lodge. It had, as an appendix, the song "For the closing of the lodge" ("Let us then with hands united . . ."). The first edition significantly calls this work "Mozart's last masterpiece . . . before his death surrounded by his closest friends." The appendix does not appear in the manuscript and is obviously not part of the cantata, which ends with a repetition of the opening chorus. We must assume that this appendix, which in time became very popular, was not by Mozart at all, but possibly (according to some scholars) by Michael Haydn. It has now become the Austrian national anthem.

The *Wiener Zeitung* printed the following announcement on January 25, 1792: "Admiration and gratitude to the departed Mozart induced a humanitarian society to publish a work by this great artist for the benefit of his widow and orphans, who are in need of help. One can justly call it his swan song. Composed with his unique talent, it was first conducted by him two days before his final illness for his closest friends. It is a cantata for the consecration of the Masonic lodge in Vienna, and the words are the work of a member of that lodge."

The *Kleine Freimaurerkantate,* scored for two tenors, one bass, two violins, viola, double-bass, flute, two oboes, and two horns, begins with an allegro chorus:

> Let our joy be blazened forth
> By the happy music's sound.

Then an instrumental introduction, with brilliant passages for the flutes and violins, leads us into a festive and exultant mood. The following solos begin with imitation; their contrapuntal style is characteristic of Mozart's more serious Masonic compositions:

> Make this place a holy temple
> By the bond of brotherhood,
> And brothers, all within your hearts,
> This day our temple sanctify.

We shall see again in the *Magic Flute* that Mozart frequently uses contrapuntal devices to accompany points of climax and tension with Masonic significance. The chorus now sings a reprise of its opening number, followed by a recitative surely sung by Adamberger:

> For the first time, noble brothers,
> We are met in this great seat of virtue and wisdom
> and truth,
> We consecrate ourselves to the sanctity of our labor,
> Which is to discover for ourselves the great mysterious
> truth.
> Joyful are all brethren on this day,
> This happy day of holy dedication
> By which the brotherhood is bound in unity.
> Let us be thankful that human kindness
> Reigns among men once again upon earth.
> Sweet will be the memories of this place
> Where every brother's heart speaks
> Of what he was and what he is,
> And what, by his endeavors, can become.
> He learns by example, shielded and cared for by
> brotherly love.
> It is here that there reigns the holiest,
> The chief, the greatest of all virtues,
> Charity, enthroned in solemn splendor.

It is possible that the rather peculiar ending of this recitative may be Schikaneder's compliment to the lodge "Zur Wohltätigkeit" (charity), to which Mozart belonged. The recitative is followed by a tenor aria, certainly also sung by Adamberger:

> Generously the godhead omnipotent
> Not in noise and pomp and clamor . . . .

and closes with a duet for tenor and bass,

> In years to come these walls shall stand
> Bearing witness to our labor.

The appendix is the song which has since become a Masonic ode: "Let us then, with hands united . . . ," scored for two tenor voices, bass, and organ accompaniment. The title is "For the closing of the lodge."

In addition to the specifically Masonic compositions Mozart also

54

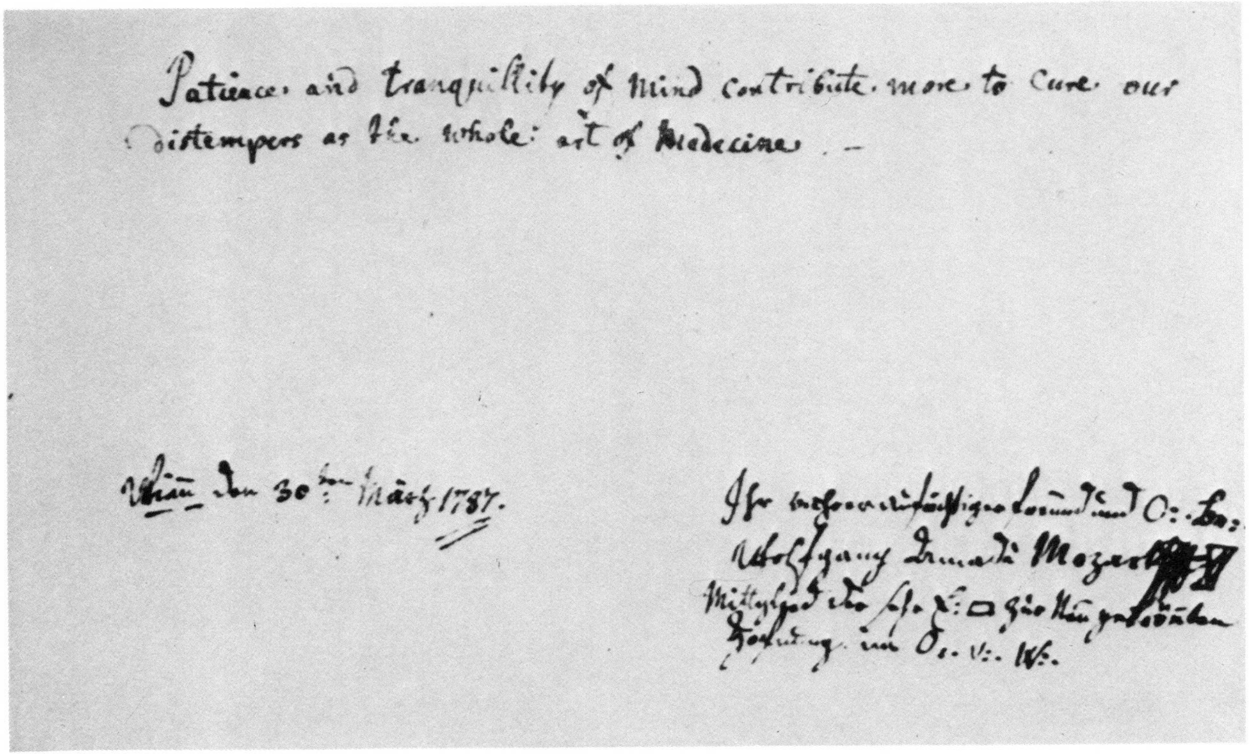

Patience and tranquillity of mind contribute more to cure our distempers as the whole art of Medecine. —

Wien den 30ten März 1787.

Ihr wahrer aufrichtiger freund und O: Br:
Wolfgang Amadè Mozart
Mitglied der sehr E: □ zur Neugekrönten
Hofnung im O: v: W:

PLATE 3.
Mozart's entry in the "Kronauer Album."

PLATE 4.

From Naudot's "Apology of Freemasons." The "Frère Américain" is supposed to be Benjamin Franklin.

composed several works which are not designated for the Craft but which are nevertheless Masonic in spirit. Foremost among these is the cantata K. 619, *Die ihr des unermesslichen Weltalls.* The words are by a merchant from Hamburg, Franz Heinrich Ziegenhagen, who, under the influence of Rousseau and the Encyclopedists, made several attempts at educational reform.

In a pamphlet, "Science of the Proper Relationships to Creation . . . ," published in Hamburg in 1792, Ziegenhagen declares that he would like to reform all existing religions and to persuade aristocrats and intellectuals to take up the study of relationships, which has advantages over all existing religions. With a view to founding a colony near Strasbourg, based on his principles, he desired to meet parents who wanted their children to devote themselves to agriculture. To us he sounds like a rationalist crank of the worst kind. He wished to propagate his ideas by aesthetic means and asked Chodowiecki for eight engravings and Mozart for a suitable song. Ziegenhagen was himself a Mason and member of the lodge "Zu den drei Schlüsseln" (three keys) in Regensburg indicating that he was probably a friend of Schikaneder's, who may have referred him to Mozart. The manuscript is now in the university library of Uppsala, where it was taken, together with sketches for the *Magic Flute,* by Silverstolpe at the beginning of the 19th century. According to a report to Breitkopf & Härtel by Niemetschek, the cantata was first performed at a "Lawyers' Academy" in Prague, on March 19, 1799. It was orchestrated by the inventor of the "orchestrion," Thomas Anton Kunz.

Ziegenhagen's science of relationships was to teach mankind to find a way to happiness by doing away with religion in favor of a natural law arising out of men's "natural" relations to one another and to nature. "Every suppressed or merely tolerated fellow human being shall become an equal member for the good of all. I speak especially of the Jews, whose condition no humanitarian can observe without pity. They would free themselves from the astrological superstitions of the Talmud and the laws of their prophets." Religious tolerance was, in fact, one of the primary conditions of Ziegenhagen. This attitude is illustrated in an engraving on the title page of the cantata, which represents a kind of Masonic lodge, with the Master in the right foreground. In the middle stands a deformed Jewish man, possibly representing Moses Mendelssohn. There is a group of ministers in the corner representing various religions, among them a Rabbi; and the inscription on the temple says: "Place yourselves in the proper relationship to each other and to the rest of creation." The "Works of Creation" are depicted in another large engraving where we see an idealized animal farm with fields, gardens, and orchards, grown-ups playing with children, in short, paradise on earth. It is unlikely that Mozart knew the contents of this pamphlet since it was published after his death.

Jahn states that there is no such thing as a Masonic style in music. But for this cantata Mozart again adopted the special atmosphere used in all his Masonic compositions, a flavor which we may designate as his "humanitarian style." To our modern ears, the text of the cantata sounds hypocritical and insincere, but the deep humanitarian feeling in the music still rings true. That Mozart was definitely thinking of Freemasonry when he composed it can be seen by the dotted rhythms of the piano accompaniment, by the tenor part, but most clearly in the melody which recalls one of the priests' scenes from the *Magic Flute*. The words undoubtedly were also influenced by Masonry. One passage, "Let strength and beauty be your aim and brightness of intellect your honor," indicates the "Three Lesser Lights" of Freemasonry, wisdom, strength, and beauty.

There is one more cantata by Mozart which may have been destined for Masonic use, *Dir, Seele des Weltalls,* K. 429. According to Köchel, it was begun in 1783, before Mozart became a Mason, but it was never completed. The humanitarian style, well-developed as it appears in his later Masonic compositions, is not yet evident. Nevertheless this work clearly shows Mozart's preoccupation with Masonic and humanitarian ideas in the years before joining the lodge.

The spirit of the cantata is related to that of Gebler's *King Thamos.* The sun worship of the Egyptians, with which Mozart was acquainted, is expressed by these words: "Oh mighty one, without thee we could not live. From thee comes fertility, warmth, and light." Since it is scored for two tenors and bass, and otherwise emphasizes the number three like the *Kleine Freimaurer-kantate* and *Maurerfreude,* it probably has Masonic significance. But its use of a large ensemble, with oboes, horns, string quartet, bassoon, and mixed chorus may have made its performance in the lodge impractical.

The *Masonic Funeral Music* for orchestra, K. 477, is one of Mozart's most important compositions. It was written around November 10, 1785, a year after Mozart's initiation, and performed at the Lodge of Mourning honoring two famous Masons, Count Esterhazy and the Duke of Mecklenburg. Esterhazy was a highly esteemed Hungarian nobleman, a Privy Councillor and high official in the government department dealing with Hungarian and Transylvanian matters, and a member of the "Crowned Hope" lodge. Georg August von Mecklenburg-Strelitz was a major-general and an affiliated member of the lodge "The Three Eagles." The ceremony took place on November 17, 1785, with an address by Brother Epstein, later printed by J. R. von Ghelen in a pamphlet which also contained another obituary for the Duke by a person associated with the lodge. The Duke had the nickname "Quin-Quin" which was used by Hugo von Hoffmannsthal in *Rosenkavalier* and recorded in a diary of Khevenhüller's known as *Aus Maria Theresias Zeit.* The number of performers required for this piece gives an indication of the importance Mozart attached to it. It is scored for string quartet, two oboes, a clarinet, three bassethorns, two horns in E flat and C, and a contra-bassoon.

The low, threatening notes of the winds anticipate the serious mood. Several chords serve as an introduction, then a plaintive, rhapsodic melody is played by the solo violin. This juxtaposition of winds and strings corresponds to the dialectic of life and inexorable death. Thus, the melody of the violin, which never really takes the firm shape of a song, is confronted by the relentless *cantus firmus* of the woodwinds. The latter is not taken verbatim from Roman Catholic liturgy but possibly from the Hebrew psalms. It must be a very ancient melody, for it is found in Persian and Italian Jewish songs. A tune in Idelsohn's *Songs of the Babylonian Jews* as well as *Jeremiah's Lamentation* are similar to it.

The string quartet, as a symbol of man struggling against his fate, fights against this *cantus firmus,* which represents the unalterable downfall of the individual. The dotted rhythms in the bass accompany the sobbing of the strings which, towards the middle of the piece, rear up in sudden anguish and then return to a gentle but serious lament. This is a true picture of death which the Mason Mozart carried in his mind when he wrote to his father for the last time on April 4, 1787. I should point out that Alfred Einstein, probably the foremost Mozart scholar of the 20th century, was not a Mason; nor was Otto Erich Deutsch. Yet Einstein attached far greater importance to the Masonic influences in Mozart's life and work than had ever been done before. One of Mozart's most important works is the great symphony in E flat, K. 543, which was finished on June 26, 1788. Einstein wrote about it in his classic book, *Mozart, his Character, his Work* (p. 234):

"We can hardly avoid the assumption of some secret Masonic meaning—less in a 'programmatic' sense than simply to find some way of explaining and characterizing this mysterious work. E-flat major is the key of the trio Mozart dedicated to his friend and helper, Puchberg. It is the key of *Die Zauberflöte*. And just as in the overture to the work the adept knocks at the gate and waits anxiously in the dark, so he does here again, until the six-four chord brings the light. The unusual song-theme of the Allegro, too, is full of those 'ties' that symbolize the brotherhood of Freemasons. Is it impossible to interpret the Andante in A-flat in the sense of that letter of 4 April 1787, addressed to Leopold, which we have quoted, with its thoughts of death, 'that best and truest friend of man,' of which the thought is 'not only no longer terrifying to me, but is indeed very soothing and consoling.' Does not this program suit well the festive character of the minuet and the cheerfulness of the Finale—a cheerfulness that reminds us only very slightly of Haydn?"

We have noted the difference between Mozart's Masonic compositions and those of earlier composers. While the latter are of a strictly functional character, Mozart's are full of the Masonic spirit. Not that Mozart was a model Mason. But instinctively he came as close as anyone to understanding the most fundamental ideas of Freemasonry which, after all, are symbols. All the compositions by Naumann, Scheibe, B. A. Weber, Ambrosch, Franz, Hurka, and all the rest are idle chatter compared to a few bars of Mozart's Masonic music. To be sure, the older pieces were usually adapted from tunes already in existence just as the melodies from the *Magic Flute* were to be adapted for Masonic songs quite soon after their creation. In 1795, *Freimaurerlieder mit Melodien,* three volumes edited by Böheim and printed by G. F. Starcke in Berlin, appeared with some material from the *Magic Flute,* additional evidence that this opera was already then assumed to be Masonic.

But the gentle and yet firm quality of Mozart's Masonic style was probably the greatest attraction. Böheim's collection begins with the song "Let Truth and Spotless Faith be Thine" sung to the tune of Papageno's song, " 'Tis love they say, love only, that makes the world go round." This text has been sung to Mozart's melody a million times by Masons and non-Masons alike. Paradoxically, it was the station identification of the largest German broadcasting station under the Nazis. It was published with an English text by Willig in Philadelphia between 1798 and 1804. The second song in Böheim's collection, a song of consecration, is sung to the music of Sarastro's aria.

Heuss described this kind of music in an essay, *Die Humanitäts-melodien im Fidelio* (humanitarian melodies in *Fidelio*). He calls it "quietly glowing with metaphysical warmth" and points out that Beethoven also used this style in his younger days. To be sure, Mozart was already approaching it before he became a Mason. But I still believe that the experience of Freemasonry was of the greatest importance in the development of this style, and that the *Magic Flute* was so successful because in it the humanitarian style was perfected.

There is no doubt that many works of Beethoven as well as those of the Romantic composers are based on this humanitarian style. We would do this music a disservice by subjecting it to mechanical analysis. Some of its characteristics are the lofty arches of the melody; large intervals; serious, song-like melodies reminiscent of old choral music; quiet, simple rhythms. A more objective description is out of the question.

THE MAGIC FLUTE: BACKGROUND[1]

IT IS REMARKABLE that at the end of his life Mozart created two masterpieces, the *Magic Flute*, which glorifies the Masonic ideal, and the *Requiem*, which expresses an acceptance of death in a way very different from that of the *Masonic Funeral Music*. The spiritual backgrounds of these works are very different: Catholicism gave birth to the *Requiem*, and the Masonic creed inspired the funeral music and the *Magic Flute*. This shows the versatility of the master, but it also demonstrates the unity of his artistic creations. The reason for this unity, the quintessence of his later years, is a preoccupation with the relationship of man to the world, a world which man himself creates, on which he is not dependent as was the thinker of the Baroque era. This was the new autonomous approach to life as it is expressed by Kant, by Goethe's *Faust*, and especially by the classical composers. Man fights against his fate. Like Beethoven in his fifth symphony, he refuses to be overwhelmed by it, he grasps it by the horns. This is Mozart's approach to God and life. To him Freemasonry is not a rational means for explaining the secret of life but rather something that helps him make his peace with fate. True, fate is created by man, but its negative side, the insignificance of the individual, is accepted as something natural and unalterable.

In order to understand the true nature of Mozart, we must not dwell too much on his demoniac side, as some musicologists like Heuss and Abert have done, but we should concentrate on the classical aspects of his nature. Only then can we see the importance of Freemasonry for him, and we will recognize the same Masonic idea in the *Requiem* and the *Magic Flute*. It is acceptance of death but not capitulation. Death does not frighten him. It does not mean entry into paradise or hell, as it did for the Baroque thinker. Mozart simply accepts death as one of the functions of existence, a less important one than life, man the individual. This

60

is the fundamental teaching of Freemasonry expressed so movingly in the initiation scenes of the *Magic Flute*.

The suggestion to write a Masonic opera may have come from Mozart's librettist DaPonte, who, several years before, had helped Mazzolà complete the text of Johann Gottlieb Naumann's Masonic opera *Osiris*. Already in that opera we can observe the struggle between good and evil, and there are some testing scenes in an Egyptian setting. But on the other hand, Mozart may spontaneously have gotten the notion of glorifying Masonry in an opera. The specific impulse to write it may have come from Schikaneder, who was a member of the Craft, but not, as was generally assumed, of Mozart's lodge.

The research of Brother Dr. Bernhard Beyer of Bayreuth has clarified Schikaneder's Masonic career. As a theatrical producer, for whom pomp and circumstance were supreme values, Schikaneder did not hesitate to get involved in transactions hardly ethical or legal, if they were to his financial advantage. A typical South German, born in Regensburg, he travelled widely and was known throughout Germany. Like many others of the 18th century, he entered the Craft for worldly reasons. His petition for admission sounds almost like the dialogue of the priests in the *Magic Flute:* "Deeply revered gentlemen,

Not curiosity or selfishness but the most sincere esteem of your exalted assembly motivates my most humble prayer for admission to your sanctuary from which, in spite of the greatest secrecy, radiates a glimmer of nobility, humanity, and wisdom. Enlighten me by your wise teachings, make me in your image, and I will remain with warmest thanks,

Your most honoring and humble servant,
Johann Emanuel Schikaneder

Regensburg, July 4, 1788."

Komorzynski points out in a biography of Schikaneder that his worst qualities were being exhibited at that time in Regensburg. He had offended public opinion by his braggadoccio, he advertised to a degree quite unheard-of in his time, and his private life gave evidence of scandal. Finally he encountered great trouble because of the dismissal of two actresses with whom he had been intimate. Public indignation about him and his private life found its way to the lodge. In the archives of the lodge "Karl zu den drei Schlüsseln" (Charles to the Three Keys) there is the following draft of a letter to Schikaneder, dated June 4, 1789:

"Excerpt from the minutes of May 4, 5789: Pleasing as the rare visits of Brother Schikaneder have been to the lodge, this matter which has been brought to court and which has become food for public gossip is strikingly unpleasant.

"It would not be in the interest of the lodge to remain indifferent in such a case. Therefore, it has been unanimously decided at this present meeting to make known to Brother Schikaneder that

"in view of the sensational occurrence he should refrain from visiting the lodge at the forthcoming St. John's festival and for the following six months.

"In order to avoid unpleasant consequences it has been deemed necessary to inform Brother Schikaneder of the decision of the lodge by this excerpt from the minutes.

By order
(signed) Hammerschmidt, Secretary."

Schikaneder, whose contract with the theater was not renewed, wanted to remain on friendly terms with the lodge. He ate humble pie and hoped that in due course enough water would flow under the bridge. He had already been passed to the second degree and decided to write an apologetic letter to the lodge:

"Most honorable and esteemed Brethren,
I hope that this case, painful though it be, will not harm me so much as to deprive me of my honest name. I laugh at the wicked people. Good ones will understand why I have acted thus and not otherwise. However, if I have committed an error which might harm the honor of the lodge, I beg the forgiveness of the entire honorable assembly.

"There are errors which are older than the honorable Craft, which I revere and into which I had the good fortune to be accepted. Honorable brethren, I submit to your wise judgment. And when I shall again know the happiness of being within your circle, I shall try to convince you all, honorable brethren, that I will behave in a manner worthy of you.

I am yours,
E. Schikaneder."

This evidence of Schikaneder's membership in the Craft is, of course, important for determining the authorship of the libretto of the *Magic Flute*. Some authorities have believed that this libretto was not written by Schikaneder at all, but by an actor living in Vienna at the time, Johann Georg Metzler, known by the name of Giesecke. This assertion was made by Julius Cornet, tenor and opera director, in a book, *Die Oper in Deutschland und das Theater der Neuzeit*, published in 1849. It was included without qualification by Otto Jahn in his biography of Mozart in 1859 and Jahn's reputation as an authority on Mozart caused its general acceptance. Cornet received the information from Giesecke himself, who was living in Vienna in 1818. Cornet was in the habit of daily meeting Seyfried and some other theatrical people in a certain Viennese restaurant. One day a distinguished-looking gentleman in a blue frock coat and white scarf introduced himself to this group as Giesecke, Professor of Mineralogy in Dublin. Only Seyfried recognized him. Cornet says that Giesecke claimed authorship of the *Magic Flute*, a matter about which Seyfried may have had some notions.

E. Dent, who did a considerable amount of research on Giesecke, is inclined to believe this. But we are justified in questioning his opinion. If Schikaneder had not been a Mason, Giesecke's claim would have better grounds. Admittedly, he was a member of the lodge "Zur neugekrönten Hoffnung" for a time, but his name does not appear in Mozart's correspondence. Through the Danish mineralogist K. J. V. Steenstrupp, who published a diary of Giesecke's travels to Greenland from 1800 to 1813 (Copenhagen, 1910), we know something of his life.

Giesecke was born in Augsburg in 1761, studied law and mineralogy at the University of Göttingen. After having acted with various theatrical companies, he appeared in Vienna in 1789. In the fall of 1789 he had begun to work for Schikaneder at the *Theater auf der Wieden*, where he remained for some time. According to Rommel, Giesecke wrote several plays in that capacity, all of them destined to fail because he had no talent as a playwright. In his fundamental study on Giesecke, Rommel draws the conclusion that his claim to authorship of the libretto was never uttered. Cornet did not say anything about Giesecke's remark for two generations after the first performance of the *Magic Flute*, or thirty years after the remark was allegedly made. None of the people whom Cornet named as having been present on that occasion ever confirmed or repeated it. Seyfried seems to have known nothing about it. One must remember that in those days, as today, teamwork was more important in the theater than individual work. It is quite possible that Giesecke, or perhaps the prompter Haselböck, gave Schikaneder some ideas which were used in the production. But certainly the conception of the work as a whole was Schikaneder's, all of this in spite of Dent's favoring Giesecke, who had become a typical Irishman.

Giesecke did, in fact, revisit Vienna in 1818, in order to sell some valuable mineralogical specimens to the imperial collection. His biography reads like a novel. In 1800 he took leave-of-absence from Schikaneder and embarked on a mineralogical expedition through Germany and Scandinavia. In Copenhagen he opened a school of mineralogy. After that he went to Greenland, living for seven years like an Eskimo, in order to study its minerals. In spite of a poor command of English, he became Professor of Mineralogy in Dublin in 1813 and received an Irish title. He sent numerous specimens to Goethe. When he suffered a stroke and died at a banquet in Dublin at the age of 72, there were several solemn obituaries and the museum was closed for a fortnight. He was a sensitive, artistic, and scholarly man, but, as we have seen, a dilettante in literature and drama who could not possibly have mustered the talent for a work like the *Magic Flute.* From what we know of his character it seems improbable that he ever made the claim. The whole matter, which has been such a force in the literature on the *Magic Flute,* is probably nothing but a piece of Viennese coffee-house gossip.

A letter written by Seyfried, now at the Mozarteum in Salzburg, sheds some interesting light on Cornet's story. It indicates that Giesecke pointed out Wieland's *Dschinnisdan* to Schikaneder, from which the latter derived the plots of several librettos. This is probably the true basis of Cornet's tale and it heralds the end of the affair Giesecke. The letter even mentions the prompter Helmböck, who also appears in Cornet's story. Cornet had said: Many people have thought that the prompter Helmböck worked with Schikaneder on the opera, but Seyfried believes that it was the prompter Haselböck who put Schikaneder's rough draft into verse form. Seyfried died in Vienna in 1848, and it strikes us as noteworthy that Cornet's book appeared the following year, when the only real witness of the incident was no longer in a position to verify it. In any case, Seyfried seems the more reliable of the two men. Cornet sounds suspect in saying that Seyfried alone knew about Giesecke's claim, while Seyfried asserts that he had heard stories about Mozart and Schikaneder from Giesecke. Moreover, Seyfried was not very fond of Schikaneder and would not have kept Giesecke's statement to himself. Even Dent does not regard Cornet as absolutely reliable. Here then is the letter:

"My esteemed friend,

"With heartfelt thanks I return the manuscript which you have entrusted to me. It gave me great pleasure, somehow making me feel younger, and it must be of historical interest to every art-lover. According to your request I am making some comments for whose reliability I am willing to vouch.

"Schikaneder made the acquaintance of Mozart, and later of Zitterbarth, in a Masonic lodge. Not the very famous one to which Born and all the literary elite of Vienna belonged, but a little bread-and-butter lodge whose members diverted themselves at the weekly meetings with music, games, and the joys of a rich table. Giesecke, who told Schikaneder about Wieland's *Dschinnis-dan* and thus provided him with the material of several of his operas, often talked to me about it. Work on the *Magic Flute* probably did not begin until the Spring of 1791, since Mozart did not spend much time on it and was generally a fast worker. He often worked at Gerl's quarters or in Sch.'s garden a few steps from the theater. I was often a guest at that table and conducted many rehearsals in that drawing-room, or, properly, shack. The prompter, Haselböck, had to write the verses on Sch.'s rough drafts and some of it may have been completely his own work, e.g. 'Good morrow, pretty maid, come tell me what's the matter' just after 'What place is this, where have I strayed?' The libretto was finished up to the first finale when *Die Zauberzither, oder Kaspar der Fagottist* (the magic zither, or Kaspar the bassoonist) appeared in Leopoldstadt. Perinet had also used Wieland's fairy tale, but had stuck closely to the original except for making it more acceptable to local taste. This worried our Emanuel considerably, but he soon thought of something, gave the whole plot a new twist, and thus improved it considerably. Had he not, Mozart would hardly have left us this wonderful, poetic, romantic swan song.

65

"Mozart visited the coronation in Frankfurt on his own initiative, in order to try to patch up his financial holes by giving concerts. When he visited Prague, in response to an invitation from the Bohemian aristocracy, all the ensemble pieces of the *Magic Flute* up to the last finale were ready, that is, vocal parts, figured bass with the main motifs written out. My cousin Henneberger was, meanwhile, working hard at rehearsing with this partial score. On his return—September 10 or 12—Mozart quickly proceeded to orchestrate and to write a few small pieces which had been omitted. On the 28th, as his own thematic catalogue indicates, the priests' march and the overture were completed. The ink was still wet when the music of the overture was brought to the dress rehearsal.

"As far as I know, Guardasoni had the opera translated into Italian in Prague in the Winter of 1793. I myself had a tight squeeze at the first performance of this *flauto magico*, which the miserly producer always called *la maladetta Zaberflute* because of its unusually lavish settings, costumes, and decorations. I remember quite vividly the tenor Benedetti as he came tripping out, calling to the pursuing snail-like monster, *Ajuto, ajuto, io sono perduto.* Bassi was very good as Papageno and Danzi an enchanting Pamina. Campi was unexcelled as Queen of the Night, but her husband Gaetano the most pitiful Sarastro I have ever seen, a real caricature.

"On the evening of December 4, when Mozart was already delirious, he imagined that he was present at a performance of the *Magic Flute* at the Wiedner theater. Almost his last words, whispered to his wife, were, 'Quiet, now Mme. Hofer is singing the high F. Now the sister-in-law is singing the second aria, "I'll have revenge . . ." How strong her B flat, how long she is holding it. Listen, listen, listen to the mother's vow.'

"The second part, *Das Labyrinth oder der Kampf mit den Elementen* (the labyrinth or the struggle with the elements) was written by Winter himself. The opera composed in conjunction with Gallus is entitled *Babylons Pyramiden.*"

In his excellent book, *Die Alt-Wiener Volkskomödie,* Otto Rommel has demonstrated convincingly that this letter was written to the librettist of *Fidelio,* Friedrich Treitschke. Treitschke wrote a novelette in the second volume of the music yearbook *Orpheus* (1841) entitled "The Magic Flute, the Village Barber, Fidelio."

Here some passages from this letter are reproduced verbatim. Apparently Treitschke had asked Seyfried, who was then about 64 and ailing, for some information to help him in writing the novelette. The following quotation from it is proof of the connection between the two men:

"The author had just finished the finale of the first scene, when the Leopoldstadt theater produced a drama most unwelcome to him, 'The Magic Zither, or Kaspar the Bassoonist.' Perinet had also used Wieland's fairy tale, but had stuck closely to the original, except for making it acceptable to local taste. This worried our Emanuel considerably, but he soon thought of something, gave the play a new twist, and thus improved it considerably. Had he not, Mozart would hardly have had enough material for his wonderful dramatic swansong."

Since Seyfried was only fifteen when the *Magic Flute* was being written, his memory must have been supplemented by retrospection. The fact that there was a sudden change in the plot is today firmly established in all the literature relating to the opera. Seyfried's letter brings us to the history of the *Magic Flute*.

Schikaneder came to Vienna in 1789, began to work as a theatrical producer, but soon found competition in Marinelli's theater for which Friedrich Hensler was writing exotic operas and Perinet, operas on supernatural subjects. Magic and oriental themes were very fashionable in Vienna at that time and, indeed, had already been featured in the days of the Venetian school of opera. Gluck's *Chinois poli en France* and Mozart's *Entführung* are well-known examples of exotic material.

In order to outdo Marinelli, Schikaneder decided first to investigate the sources from which Hensler and Perinet were drawing their material. His first "magic opera," *Der Stein der Weisen oder die Zauberinsel* (the sages' stone or the magic isle), with music by Schack, was performed in 1790. The material came from Wieland's fairy tale, *Dschinnisdan*. This opera was again performed in 1804, and Komorzynski gives a list of the characters taken from contemporary reviews. There was one good and one evil genius, an innocent couple whose love encounters many obstacles, a humorous character with a happy-go-lucky wife, and an underworld ruler called Eutifronte. There is no question but that it is a precursor of the *Magic Flute*. On March 7, 1791, in order to save himself from financial ruin, Schikaneder asked Mozart to compose an opera for him using the story "Lulu or the Magic Flute" from the third volume of *Dschinnisdan*. Mozart, who knew Schikaneder from Salzburg, agreed and began composing. They had progressed as far as the first finale when a dramatization of the same fairy tale entitled *Kaspar der Fagottist* was produced at the Leopoldstadt theater, with music by Wenzel Müller. Forced to change the plot, Schikaneder introduced Masonic themes. All of this is the generally accepted origin of the *Magic Flute*, but in order to interpret the facts properly we must return to Giesecke.

According to Komorzynski, Giesecke may have given Schikaneder another supernatural libretto, *Oberon, König der Elfen*, at the beginning of 1791. It was performed on May 6, with music by Wranitzky. Thus, Schikaneder must have known it when he asked Mozart to collaborate in March of that year. In Giesecke's opera a young knight and his page, Scherasmin, abduct the beautiful Amanda from the sultan's palace. The knight is also accompanied by Oberon, who gives him a magic horn to ward off danger. The comical Fatme becomes the girl-friend of Scherasmin. All this is based on the fairy tale "Lulu" in *Dschinnisdan,* in which a sorcerer steals the "radiant fairy's" daughter and also the "golden ray of fire." A prince is sent to rescue her. The radiant fairy has given him a ring which enables him to take on any appearance he wishes, and a magic flute which can influence people's passions. Disguised as an old musician, he enters the villain's seraglio and rescues the beauty. The sorcerer is doomed to everlasting flight before the victorious fairy. Scherasmin is given to the prince as a companion. Oberon's horn corresponds to the magic flute in Mozart's work, and to Papageno's pipe. The fairy becomes the Queen of the Night and the sorcerer is turned into a lustful moor. The princess's portrait is given the hero to persuade him to embark on the rescue mission.

Mozart and Schikaneder began working together at the inn on the Kahlenberg and a summer-house in the courtyard of the Freihaus, the same house which now stands on the Kapuzinerberg in Salzburg. Then came June 8, 1791, and Perinet's dramatization of the fairy tale "Lulu," *Kaspar der Fagottist,* was produced. It is assumed that Schikaneder's plot was suddenly changed at this point, but we shall probably never be sure. Perhaps both Mozart and Schikaneder suddenly became aware of its triviality which became all the more apparent in the company of Müller's music.

What had already been composed, that is, everything up to the first finale, was left intact, but from there on the story is said to have been changed. The good queen suddenly becomes a vindictive woman, the three genii, whom she herself had sent, suddenly become associated with the other side, with the worshippers of light and Sarastro, their high priest. It is possible, as Komorzynski indicated, that the tests by fire and water were originally to be passed by the wicked sorcerer, like those in *Zelnor und Eremide,* which was performed in Munich in 1782. This is the basis of Jahn's theory of a sudden break in the history of the *Magic Flute.* But in reality there was no such break.

Tests and trials were very common in 18th century literature. In Wieland's *Stein der Weisen* a magician describes his descent into the great pyramid in Memphis to be initiated into the mysteries. In order to prove his worthiness he had to pass several tests, first to swim across a raging torrent and then to walk on a narrow path through a sea of flames, whereupon the God of Holy Silence imparted the solution of the mystery (Komorzynski). Wieland, in turn, may have derived this motif from Terrasson's novel *Sethos,* to which we shall return presently. He had been interested in the occult for a long time but did not become a Mason until 1809. He may not have understood the Masonic ideas in *Sethos,* which were beyond the capacity of uninitiated persons and were not used in *Dschinnisdan.*

There is another opera which seems to have considerably influenced the work of Mozart and Schikaneder, *Das Sonnenfest der Brahminen* (the sun festival of the Brahmins) by Hensler, performed by Marinelli's company on Sept. 9, 1790. The plot is taken from Kotzebue's *Sonnenjungfrau* (sun maiden) and deals with an Englishman and an Indian girl. There are assemblies of priests, temple scenes, hymns to Brahma, and, at the end, the temple of the sun. The symbol of the sun appears between rows of columns, surrounded by sparkling stars.

Thamos, König von Aegypten by Gebler, for which Mozart had composed the music in 1780, is a further source of material for the *Magic Flute.* In the temple of the sun at Heliopolis, decorated with a golden symbol of the sun, the banished King Menes reigns as high priest. He has taken the name of Sethos and watches over the love between his daughter, Tharsis, and Thamos, whose father has usurped Menes's throne and banished him. Thamos expects to be king when his father dies. He has a confidant, Pheron, who is also in love with Tharsis and hopes to become king of Egypt with her as his queen. Aided at first by the sun priestess, the malicious Mirza, he conspires against Thamos. But Sethos, disclosing his true identity, uncovers the conspiracy. Thamos and Tharsis become king and queen, Pheron and Mirza are punished by death.

The opera *Osiris* by Naumann has been neglected as a source for the *Magic Flute*. We know already that its composer was a Mason and composed a number of Masonic songs. He intended *Osiris* to be his great testimonial in behalf of Freemasonry, much as Mozart and Schikaneder conceived the *Magic Flute* to be theirs. Here, too, the sun-worship of the Egyptians is essential. Orus, like Tamino, must face all sorts of dangers before he can win Aretea, the embodiment of virtue. In the manner of the first draft of the *Magic Flute*, Aretea has fallen into the hands of a wicked sorcerer. Osiris, King of Egypt, gives her picture to Orus and bids him to be steadfast. The aria *Oh, cara vista* is similar to Tamino's aria, sung upon seeing Pamina's portrait, "Oh, loveliness beyond compare."

All of this has a mythological background. Osiris, King of Egypt and protector of civilization, is opposed by Typhon, who represents evil. A struggle ensues between Typhon's son, Geron, and Osiris's son, Orus, both in love with Aretea, who is under the protection of Isis. Note the similarity to *Thamos,* in which the prince and Tharsis grow up under the guidance of Menes. The end of the opera is parallel to both the *Magic Flute* and *Thamos:* Annihilation of the forces of darkness, a change of scene, a grand finale in the temple of the sun.[2]

Osiris had a model in Naumann's Swedish opera, *Cora och Alonzo* (1782). Its libretto, by G. G. Adlerbeth, was taken from Marmontel's novel, *Les Incas.* This opera became very popular, especially after a piano arrangement was published in Germany in 1780. Incidentally, this piano score and the preface to it were prepared by Mozart's friend in Dresden, Johann Leopold Neumann. Engländer has pointed out that this opera, although it deals with the consecration of Peruvian priests for the service of the sun, contains Masonic choruses similar to the songs which Naumann was composing at the time. As one example, the aria, *Du heilige Quelle reiner Seelen* (Oh holy spring of pure souls) is a forerunner of "Oh, Isis and Osiris," even in the details of the orchestral accompaniment. Again, the high priest's recitative on p. 67 of the piano score, *Du wirst den Strahlengott nun schauen* (Now you will see the radiant god) is reminiscent of the priests' scenes in the *Magic Flute*, the dotted notes in the bass may be Masonic elements, and as Tamino seeks his Pamina and follows her through the horrors of wilderness, Alonzo searches for Cora. This quest is represented by a ballet in Naumann's second scene. Alonzo and the priestesses come out of their dwellings and perform a pantomimic dance which expresses horror and confusion. Alonzo paces back and forth, distraught because he does not see Cora among them. As, in the *Magic Flute's* 32nd scene, Tamino asks, "Oh voice of mystery, lives then Pamina still?" Alonzo demands of the invisible priestesses, "Is Cora dead? Where is she? Where?" The choir answers, "Stranger, thou seekest news in vain." It seems to me that the scenes between Alonzo and Cora must have profoundly influenced Mozart and Schikaneder. This is also true of the character of Zulma, a counterpart to the Queen of the Night. Note the recitative of Alonzo, "Tyrannical woman, whom even heaven must condemn." Perhaps Mozart saw this opera on his Dresden sojourn, if indeed he did not already know the piano score. His letter from Dresden, written on April 13, 1789, describes a visit which he paid to Neumann, where he saw Mme. Duschek again. After breakfast he heard a mass by Naumann in the court chapel conducted by the composer. Mozart thought this work mediocre.

This, then, was the background of Mozart and Schikaneder when they set out to turn fairy tale into opera. From here on it was only a short distance to the genuinely Masonic ritual through which the *Magic Flute* became a drama of more than local and timely importance. In order to integrate all the sources, we must turn to one more work which influenced the *Magic Flute,* especially the fashioning of the priests' scenes. It is Terrasson's novel, *Sethos.*

In 1837, Eduard Duller had already pointed to *Sethos* as one of the sources in an essay, *Ein Rückblick auf die Quellen des Gedichtes zur Zauberflöte* (a review of the sources of the libretto for the *Magic Flute*). Later scholars began to neglect this novel, until Dent once more pointed out its importance.[3]

The author, Abbé Jean Terrasson, Professor of Greek at the

Collège de France, was born in Lyons in 1670 and died in Paris in 1750. *Sethos* is the only well-known book among his writings on the history of philosophy. It was published in 1731 and entitled *Sethos, histoire du vie tirée des monuments anecdotes de l'ancienne Egypte. Traduite d'un manuscrit Grec.* Several German translations appeared, beginning with one by Wend, published in Hamburg in 1732, under the title, *Abriss der wahren Heldentugend des Sethos, König von Aegypten* (sketch of the true heroic virtue of Sethos, King of Egypt).

The definitive translation, however, is by Matthias Claudius, published in Breslau by Gottlieb Löwe (vol. 1, 1777, vol. 2, 1778) with the title *Geschichte des aegyptischen Königs Sethos* (story of the Egyptian King Sethos).

This novel was a great influence in French Freemasonry as the basis of the Misraim cult which uses the Egyptian ritual. This cult was founded by individuals who, like the writers J. L. Laurence, Marie Alexandre Lenoir, and Reghellini de Schio, found the roots of Masonry in ancient Egypt. Egyptology was then very fashionable in France because of Napoleon's expedition. *Sethos* continued to play a role in Freemasonry to the end of the 19th century. The famous Egyptologist, Lenoir, was mainly concerned with the connection between the ancient Egyptian religions and Freemasonry. He is responsible for establishing this relationship as part of the Masonic heritage.

Throughout the 18th century these matters were the subject of much speculation. In the first issue of the *Journal für Freymäurer*, Ignaz von Born dealt with the mysteries of the Egyptians in an essay in which he, like Terrasson, referred to the writings of Diodorus Siculus. This Roman historian, a contemporary of Julius Caesar and Augustus, was the author of a world history whose first volume was devoted to the Egyptians. Besides Diodorus and Plutarch, Lucius Apuleius, born 125 A.D., influenced our opera. The initiation ritual and several other details seem ultimately to be based, at least partially, on his *Metamorphoses.*

Another very early source is the third century novel, *Aethiopica,* by Heliodorus. It deals with the very involved fates of two lovers, Theagenes and Chariclea, who, like Tamino and Pamina, undergo difficult tests and are finally consecrated as priests. Particulars about the connections between the *Magic Flute* and 18th century Egyptology can be found in *Die Zauberflöte, eine Studie zum*

Lebenszusammenhang Aegypten-Antike-Abendland by Siegfried Morenz (Köln, 1952). Morenz traces the names Pamina and Tamino to Egyptian origins. Unfortunately, Schikaneder was mistaken in naming them. Their names should have been Pamino and Tamina, since Pa-min indicates the male, and Ta-min the female, belonging to Min, a local god of Coptos and Achmin, the patron of the Eastern desert of Egypt.

About the time of Born's publication on the mysteries of the Egyptians there appeared a small booklet, *Crata repoa, oder die Einweihung in der alten geheimen Gesellschaft der egyptischen Priester (Crata repoa,* or the initiation into the ancient secret society of Egyptian priests), printed in 1785 (no place of publication given). Although he seems to have derived a certain amount of inspiration from it, Born refers to this anonymous publication with some contempt. A closer examination of those parts of Terrasson's book which bear on Masonry and have played a part in the creation of the *Magic Flute* may help us to appreciate the relationship among all these writings.

Queen Dalucca, undoubtedly a relative of the Queen of the Night, seizes the throne after the death of Queen Nephte, and establishes a reign of tyranny and retribution. Meanwhile, Sethos, the rightful king, grows up under the wise guidance of his tutor, Amedes, and is initiated by him into the mysteries of Egyptian priesthood. In our opera, Sarastro is cast in the mold of the high priest, whose sayings at the funeral of Queen Nephte are full of wisdom. The funeral procession, which reminds us of Sarastro's triumphal entry, is described in great detail:[4]

"Daylight was shut off from the entrance of the palace, which was illuminated with lamps. A gilt carriage with four wheels was placed under the entrance. On the carriage was the queen's throne with three steps leading up to it, and above the throne a golden crown set with many precious stones, borne by a golden sphinx with spread wings. The carriage had two shafts and was drawn by 14 horses splendidly harnessed as for a triumphal procession.

"The high priest of Memphis, who was to present the dead queen to her judges, was carried behind her in an open coffin, dressed in white, with a veil over his face, in the position of a deceased. The rest of the priests walked behind them in two single files of about 500 each and separated by a distance equal to the width of the road. They were uniformly dressed, veiled, in one hand carried an augur staff bent at the top and in the other a ring or compass of gold from which a piece of rope was suspended."

The dead queen is to be taken before a tribunal, a choir of priests, who were to judge her and decide whether she was worthy of being admitted to the gods. "The tribunal is seated on 41 chairs forming two semi-circular rows, placed on a wide platform with twelve steps leading up to it. They wore tunics or white vests, as priests and initiates, and over these the wide, red cloaks of judges. Each wore a golden chain with a sapphire engraved with the figure of truth suspended from it.[5] They sat in the following order: the high priest, chief of the senate, sat on a raised chair in the middle of the semi-circle, and on each side sat the two initiates, judges named in Memphis, of which Amedes was the first. Beside them sat 16 'Priests of the Labyrinth,'[6] and then 22 initiates chosen by the others."

This explains the number of priests, 18, at the beginning of the second act of the *Magic Flute*. Abert's explanation[7] of this number as twice three-times-three is probably in error. According to Masonic tradition, 18 priests kept watch over Hiram's grave, and the number of priestesses who performed the sacrifices in *Sethos* (p. 281) is also 18. The high priest's announcement that all those present were now to present any well-founded accusations against the dead one has a truly Masonic ring. The decision as to whether the queen is to be admitted among the immortals is to be based on examination.

"The judges throw small pieces of white paper into the 'dreadful urn,' the mere thought of which makes the ancient kings observe justice." Even palms appear in the novel. Sethos and the priests, as well as the initiates, carry palm branches in the triumphal procession; in the *Magic Flute* this is done by the three genii. The following passage from the high priest's funeral oration is remarkable. It deals with the Queen:

"The thought of revenge never entered her mind. She left it to ordinary people to practice hatred." We may well assume that this passage inspired Sarastro's aria, "We know no thought of vengeance." The work stresses descriptions of the priests' costumes. At public processions they are blue, purple, or red and cover the head. This is reminiscent of the blue used in Craft lodges and the red of the Royal Arch. In the *Magic Flute*, the priests signify assent by blowing trombones. In the novel, the dead queen's carriage is announced by shawms and oboes, alternating at regular intervals with trumpets and drums.

The new initiates wear "tunics, trains, and veils, swords in their hilts, red and gold colored sashes and crowns of myrtle and palm leaves." The palm leaves may be the counterpart of the sprig of acacia in the Masonic ritual. Schikaneder, however, has put the palm branches in the hands of the three genii. They replace the three priests of Terrasson who "appear now grave, now serene, and encourage the neophyte to observe silence in the company of women." In both novel and opera, two priests, "wearing a veil that reaches down to their chests," lead the neophyte. It is, however, the descriptions of the tests themselves which had the greatest impact on the *Magic Flute*.

The entrance of the labyrinth is at the North. While discussing ethical problems, Amedes and Sethos are secretly watched by the priests. The neophytes are led by an initiated guide. The words of Amedes to Sethos give us an indication of Schikaneder's conception of the setting for the tests. "My son, you see to the North a door by which we entered and by which we could leave again. You see another door to the East which leads to a path running parallel to the archways which are still closed to you." This path was six feet wide, very even, and in a semi-circle. A warrior six feet tall stood on each side. As Sethos tried to enter he noticed on one archway the following inscription in black letters:

"WHOEVER WALKS THIS PATH ALONE WITHOUT LOOKING BEHIND HIM SHALL BE PURIFIED BY FIRE, WATER, AND AIR, AND IF HE CAN OVERCOME HIS FEAR OF DEATH HE SHALL EMERGE FROM THE BOWELS OF THE EARTH INTO DAYLIGHT, AND HE SHALL THEN HAVE THE RIGHT TO PREPARE HIS SOUL FOR RECEIVING THE SECRETS OF THE GREAT GODDESS ISIS."

A comparison of this inscription to the song of the Armored Men shows the extent to which Schikaneder has drawn from Claudius's translation of *Sethos:*

75

Who treads the path of toil that unto wisdom leadeth
His soul the purge of fire and water needeth.
When him the awful fear of death no more can fright
Then may he rise to gain the sacred light.
There with the enlightened shall he take his place
To know the mystic rites of Isis face to face.

The two now set out, Sethos walking ahead, Amedes wearing a helmet-like lamp on his head. They reach a square window. If the candidate loses courage the priest is to take him back to the entrance and exact a promise to keep his experiences secret. Sethos is amazed at the length of the path. Walking a considerable distance, "they come to a locked iron door on the right, that is, the South side. Two steps further they see three men with helmets and the head of the god Anubis. One of them addresses the candidate:

" 'We are not here to bar your way. Continue if the gods have given you courage. But if you should want to turn back later, we shall hinder you. Now there is still time to turn back, but hereafter, unless you continue on your way without shrinking or looking back, you can never leave this place again.' Sethos passes on, and at the end of the path he sees the faint glow of a flame. Doubling his pace, he arrives at a vaulted chamber in which two huge fires are burning; the smoke escapes through some pipes in the ceiling from which the flames are deflected downwards, giving the room the appearance of a red-hot oven." Between the two fires Sethos sees "a grill of red-hot iron, eight feet wide and thirty feet long." He walks across the grill and thus passes his trial by fire. His trial by water consists of having to swim across a raging torrent, holding a burning torch in his hand. The last of Sethos's tests is one of mechanical skill, no trace of which can be found in the opera.

After Sethos has passed all his tests he comes to a room which is "brilliantly illuminated by daylight or, at night-time, by lamps." He is received by the priests ranged in two rows in the sanctum. He gets a drink of water from the river Lethe which will help him "to forget all the maxims he has learned from the uninitiated." The high priest then tells him to stand in front of the statue of Isis, Osiris, and Orus, and says, "Oh, Isis, goddess of the Egyptians, give your spirit to your new servant who has braved so many dangers for your sake. Let him find the riches of his

76

soul and teach his heart your law so that he will be worthy of knowing your secrets." The *Magic Flute* has a corresponding passage:

Oh hear us, Isis and Osiris!
For these that seek your light we pray,
In all their perils grant them patience
And lead them safe in wisdom's way!
Let them draw near without denial;
Or if too frail to stand their trial,
Their youthful ardor call to mind,
So may they life eternal find.

The musical structure of this aria is also related to Terrasson's description. In the novel, all the priests repeat the first words of the prayer; Mozart parallels this by having the priests' chorus repeat the last line of each stanza of Sarastro's aria.

The inscription over the doorway, "He who walks this path alone . . . ," seems to have made such a deep impression on Mozart and Schikaneder that the scene with the two Armored Men has been turned into something almost super-human. But Abert is mistaken in saying that the words of their song are similar in style to those of contemporary Masonic songs. This is out of the question, since the lodge lyrics never went beyond everyday thoughts. The importance assigned to this scene in the novel caused the librettist to place it in a strategic spot. As in the *Masonic Funeral Music,* Mozart here uses a polyphonic setting, and the figured chorale is a picture of the darkness of human fate at whose end is only death. The ostinato motif, taken from an old chorale, like the *cantus firmus* in the *Funeral Music,* reminds us that we cannot escape our fate.

If a candidate failed any of the three tests he could not return to the upper world for the rest of his life. He was then seized by three men, "servants of the second degree," who took him to a subterranean temple from which he could never return to the surface of the earth. This was done in order to assure the secrecy of the mysteries. Unsuccessful candidates, the initiates of the second degree, lived pleasantly in this captivity and could even marry if they wished. It is highly probable that Mozart and Schikaneder had these unsuccessful ones in mind when creating the Papageno scenes. He, too, undergoes the tests, but cannot make the grade and is satisfied with food, drink, and Papagena. There is a clear distinction between the initiates, who strive for purity of the soul, and the others for whom worldly existence is all.

The frequent thunderclaps in the *Magic Flute* also have their model in *Sethos*. In the third test, "the noise of the wheels in the darkness is fully as dreadful as death itself." This noise also served as a warning signal for the priests in the sanctum who were waiting for the new initiate. They instantly closed all windows and openings through which the people in the temple could look in. The common people knew nothing of these hidden machines and imagined that the noise was a thunderstorm, unleashed by a god as a signal that he wished to communicate with the priests.

The next portion may also have influenced Mozart and Schikaneder. According to it, Orpheus came to Egypt from Thrace in order to be initiated, failed the tests, but was admitted as a special favor. Euridyce was stung by an insect and died. Orpheus found the entrance to the underworld, and when he read the inscription on the doorway he imagined that passing the tests and being initiated would enable him to find Euridyce and to lead her back from the world of spirits. He passed the fire and water tests. When he failed the third one, he took his lyre, determined to die. But the priests were merciful because of his art, granted him admission to the temple and reunited him with Euridyce.

We also find the Orpheus motif in the *Magic Flute*. Obviously, Tamino's flute is the counterpart of Orpheus's lyre, but more important, we have the combination of love for a woman and desire for initiation, a combination which is not found in other dramatic works of the period. This circumstance alone is sufficient justification for calling *Sethos* the most important single source of the *Magic Flute*.

The initiation of women is an important theme in the literature of that time. Heliodorus, although stating that women were barred from sacred ceremonies in principle, already relates the case of one noble lady of outstanding character for whom, like Pamina, an exception was made. Schikaneder drew all his information on esoteric matters from Ignaz von Born's essay, mentioned above, which is based on the writings of Diodorus Siculus and refers to *Sethos*. He may also have heard some of the many circulating stories about female Masons. The question was constantly being discussed in German literature. In 1785, Wieland wrote in

Teutscher Merkur that, "as far as women were concerned, Free-masons were willing to open their hearts but not their lodges." When Goethe's son, August, was a guest at a ladies' night of the lodge "Amalia" in Weimar and was asked to express their thanks to the lodge, his father wrote a humorous verse for the occasion:

> *Sollen aber wir, die Frauen*
> *Dankbar solche Brüder preisen*
> *Die ins Innere zu schauen*
> *Immer uns zur Seite weisen?*

which may be freely translated as

> Why, oh why, should we, the women
> Grateful to those brothers be
> Who cannot perform their duties
> When in our company?

Herder, in his Masonic writings, also dealt with this question, which was being discussed throughout Europe. Goldoni satirized the exclusion of women from lodges in a comedy, *Donne Curiose* (curious women).

During the 18th century, the so-called Lodges-of-Adoption, into which both men and women were admitted, began to spring up in France. The famous lodge "Les neuf soeurs," the lodge of Voltaire, had its own Lodge of Adoption over which presided Mme. Helvétius, wife of the French philosopher and *litterateur* Claude Adrien Helvétius. In 1781 Queen Marie Antoinette said about these lodges, *Tout le monde en est.*

There are many stories about the admission of women into regular lodges. One of the most famous is about Mrs. Elizabeth Aldworth, daughter of Arthur St. Leger, Viscount Doneraile, who inadvertently entered the lodge in her father's company. Since she had unintentionally heard part of the ceremony she was initiated in order to guard the Masonic secret. Thackeray tells this humorous story in *My Grandfather's Time*. At this point we should mention the so-called *Mopsorden* of which both men and women were members. As a matter of fact, the exclusion of women was never put to strict practice, *viz.* the French *Le Droit humain* and the American Order of the Eastern Star.

The duet "man and wife, wife and man approach divinity," points to the high ideals of love and humanism which are most persuasively expressed in Masonry. The final secret of the Craft is symbolized by the Hebrew password, *Makbenak* (he lives within the son). It represents the principle of resurrection and regeneration, symbolized by the initiation which in its most lofty form is shown in the *Magic Flute*.

To return to *Sethos*, there are even more parallels to the *Magic Flute*. The candidate must fast for 81 days (nine times nine, the Masonic triad) and is allowed only water to drink. At the end of the fast he is rewarded with a light meal and a glass of excellent wine (Papageno's drinking scene). Even the serpent appears in the novel, but it is a monster which consumes whole herds of cattle. It is killed by Sethos at the beginning of the novel, instead of the three ladies. There are other parallels which we cannot discuss here.

Schikaneder may have used yet some other sources for creating his Egyptian setting. Ferdinand Josef Schneider, in his book, *Die Freimaurerei und ihr Einfluss auf die geistige Kultur in Deutschland*, points out a number of such writings from the end of the 18th century. Did they stimulate the creation of the opera, or was it the *Magic Flute* which aroused people's interest in ancient Egypt?

A novel by Fr. Eberhard Rambach, published in Zerbst in 1793 and entitled *Aylo und Dschandina oder die Pyramiden*, describes a society aiming at universal happiness. *Geheimnisse der alten Egypzier* by Christian Heinrich Spiess, published in Leipzig in 1798, describes the "irresistible longing" for Egypt, the land of ancient secret wisdom. Here two boys become "victims of envious relatives." Schneider shows that initiated women play an important part in the esoteric novels of the late 18th century. We can only completely appreciate the *Magic Flute* if we see it against a background of the contemporary fiction which abounds with ghosts, knights, and robbers.

Though for the initiated there can be no doubt about the essentially Masonic nature of the *Magic Flute,* many students have been unaware of this aspect of the work. Even in today's literature several studies of this masterpiece dismiss its Masonic implications with a passing reference. Ever since it was first performed, this opera has been assigned interpretations of the most diverse kinds.

These interpretations are the subject of a study by Blümml,

published in the first volume of the *Mozart-Jahrbuch,* entitled *Ausdeutungen der Zauberflöte* (interpretations of the *Magic Flute*). At the beginning there were two schools of thought, one revolutionary, one conservative. The Masonic interpretation did not appear until later, but it won the day. Blümml is quick to admit that it has long been accepted, even though "it is more speculative than objective."

Already political bias tended to encroach on scholarly objectivity. In 1817, the revolutionary interpretation was well known in the Rhineland even before Franz Gräffer asserted it in *Josephinische Curiosa.* According to his view, the opera's background is the liberation of the French people from the shackles of despotism through the wisdom of a better government. The Queen of the Night represents the despotic rule of Louis XIV, Pamina personifies freedom, the daughter of tyranny, Tamino is the people. The three ladies are the deputies of the Three Estates, Sarastro stands for the wisdom of better government. The priests are the national assembly, Papageno represents the rich, Monostatos the *emigrés,* Papagena, equality, etc. We are reminded of George Bernard Shaw's satirical interpretation of Richard Wagner's operas. Even the wild animals are said to represent the coats-of-arms of various countries, the lion representing Holland, the leopard England, and the eagle the Holy Alliance.

But we can also reverse the charges. While the revolutionary interpretation fitted the progressive Rhinelanders, Mozart seemed to the Austrian reactionaries of the Metternich era a man of exemplary honesty who virtuously upheld the established order. In 1794, in a weekly paper published in Linz, *Göttergespräche gegen die Jakobiner* (speeches of the gods against the Jacobins), the *Magic Flute* is described as a bulwark against the French Revolution. Representing France, Pamina receives a prince, Tamino, and is rescued from the unhappy fate of a republic. Papageno, the bird-catcher, lures people into the Jacobin Club where he will imprison them and hand them over to the Queen of the Night, that is, the republican government. Here, too, art is subverted by specious political allegory.

Significantly, it was not in Austria, where Freemasons had been persecuted since the death of Joseph II, but in Northern Germany, that the Masonic interpretation first appeared in writing. Since in Prussia Masons had never been persecuted it was natural that the Masonic traditions surrounding the *Magic Flute* should settle there. Ludwig von Batzko, the blind historian, attended a Königsberg performance of the opera in 1794, which proved a profound experience for him. His allegorical interpretation was published in *Journal des Luxus und der Moden* IX, in an essay entitled *Allegorie aus der Zauberflöte.*

Blümml points out that Batzko's explanation is based on that simple formula, the age-old struggle between light and darkness, good and evil, enlightenment and superstition, thus preparing the way for later interpretations in the specifically Masonic sense. Batzko makes no absolute assertions about Masonry, but only points out "that some scenes allude to the ceremonies of certain orders. Their members will recognize them without explanation, and even the uninitiated will understand part of them provided they are acquainted with the mysteries of the ancient cultures. But for those who are ignorant of these it would take too long to explain the individual allusions and expressions."

Leopold von Sonnleithner (1797-1873) was the first non-Mason to see the opera as a glorification of Freemasonry. In an essay on the *Magic Flute* written in 1857,[8] he points out that after the end of the first scene, "Schikaneder introduced a new subject which does not appear in Joachim Perinet's operetta, *Kaspar der Fagottist,* although the same source was used for both works. This subject, a glorification of Freemasonry, created some discrepancies between the first and second acts." Sonnleithner was old enough to know a number of contemporaries of Mozart and Schikaneder, and he may also have been acquainted with Seyfried,[9] who probably told him about the great days of Freemasonry in Vienna. His essays were presumably written at the request of Otto Jahn, the great Mozart biographer who was the first to advocate a purely Masonic interpretation of the *Magic Flute.*

But Blümml completely omits the most important document; the original printing of the libretto in 1791 proves, beyond a shadow of doubt, that Schikaneder, and of course also Mozart, were thinking of nothing other than Freemasonry in creating their masterpiece. This is obvious even on the title page which depicts the entrance of the temple. A five-pointed star, symbol of the second degree, is suspended, and on the lower right are those of the first degree, square and trowel, and an hour-glass representing the third. We shall return later to those parts of the text which are specifically rooted in the ritual.[10]

For years now the opera's Masonic meaning has been generally, if not indisputably, accepted. Years after its creation, Friedrich Daumer, writer and philosopher, was the first to see in it a Masonic allegory. After becoming a Roman Catholic convert, he cast scorn and suspicion on the Craft in the manner of Eduard Emil Eckert, the well-known pamphleteer and enemy of Freemasonry. In the fourth issue of his periodical, *Aus der Mansarde,* (from the attic), Daumer attacked the Masons, showing himself a member of Eckert's bandwagon. But his investigations of the activities of secret societies did lead him to see the connection between Freemasonry and the *Magic Flute* which he presented in his periodical. To him, Sarastro represented the spiritual light, a secular priest or a worldly ruler; the Queen of the Night was superstition, Monostatos was "a frightening and distorted caricature of the old-fashioned Catholic clergy." The three ladies are either the three religions (Christianity, Islam, and Judaism) or the three branches of Christianity.

Another supporter of the Masonic interpretation was Moritz Alexander Zille. A Freemason and preacher at the university church in Leipzig, he became editor of the *Allgemeine Zeitung für Christentum und Kirche* in 1846. In his strictly Deistic views he was a sincere Freemason. His conception of Christianity was that of a warm, bright, optimistic religion, whose humaneness exceeded mere tolerance. With this conviction, he founded a society, *Kirchlicher Verein für alle Religions-bekenntnisse* (church society for all religious faiths). When the representatives of the German nation were assembled in Frankfurt in 1848, this group petitioned them in behalf of separation of church and state, and freedom of worship for all religions.

Among Zille's many writings, some of which were published in the *Freimaurerzeitung,* whose editor he became in 1852, is an interpretation of the *Magic Flute.* It appeared in 1866 with the title *Die Zauberflöte, Texterläuterung für alle Mozart Verehrer.* His interpretation is summarized in two sentences by Blümml. It is based on Jahn's suggestions and fuses them into a systematic theory. As an historian, he is struck by the fact that the opera was composed at a time when Masons were being persecuted by Emperor Leopold who had succeeded Joseph II.

"Mozart and Schikaneder, in creating the *Magic Flute*, performed a deed of valor, for in spite of the disapproval of the higher-ups they defended their noble cause. It is, therefore, the swan song of Masonry in Austria, an eloquent defense of those who were innocently condemned, a farewell worthy of those who were exiled, but also a magic means for Freemasonry to continue spreading in spite of all prohibitions."

Zille attempted to identify the characters as leaders of Austrian Masonry. In Sarastro he recognizes Ignaz von Born, famous Freemason and scholar, the hub of all intellectual life in Vienna, who has been a central figure throughout this volume. The reader will remember that when Theodor of Bavaria began his persecutions of Masons, Born returned all of his Bavarian diplomas with a letter stating his convictions on the subject. Evidently Masons felt quite secure in Austria at that time, and the changes after Joseph's death were a great blow. But Masonry again raised its head in the *Magic Flute*.

The other characters also had historical counterparts. In the Queen of the Night, Zille recognized Empress Maria Theresia, who hated the Craft so much that she detailed soldiers to surround the house in which her husband, Francis of Lorraine, was attending a Masonic meeting. Tamino is Joseph II, Pamina the Austrian people, and Monostatos stands for popery and monasticism.

Several authors support Zille's interpretation; among them is Dent, who differs only in respect to Monostatos, whom he believes to be Leopold Aloys Hoffmann, that traitor to the Craft who, after the outbreak of the French Revolution, dedicated his life to persecuting Freemasonry. But Hoffmann's anti-Masonic writings did not begin appearing until 1792, somewhat too late for him to find a place in the opera.

As the Masonic conception of the *Magic Flute* began to spread, a reaction against it set in. Schurig sees in it a purely personal statement of Mozart's beliefs, unrelated to Freemasonry, and Blümml congratulates him for finally having freed himself from the Masonic interpretation. He tries to prove his point by calling the overture an adaptation of a sonata by Clementi, a vague and irrelevant statement. Some bigoted Christian writers could not forgive Mozart for being a Mason and including Masonic material in the *Magic Flute*.

Josef Kreitmaier calls the *Magic Flute* libretto unimaginative and prosaic, "a welcome piece of propaganda for Freemasons." But he asserts that Mozart remained religious in spite of his Masonic allegiance and the thought of opposing the Roman Catholic church was contrary to his beliefs.

There were several writers, enemies of Masonry, who regarded Mozart's lodge membership as discreditable. In a lecture, *Mozart und das Christentum in der Musik* (Mozart and Christianity in music), given on December 13, 1891, Dr. Albert Wiesinger says of the *Funeral Music:* "The Freemasons gave Mozart a ridiculous build-up, but they let him die hungry and poor." In order to deliver a blow to Masonry, these people did not stop at lying. A newspaper article reported the following as historical fact: "When Mozart saw that the Austrian lodges were nothing but ridiculous tomfoolery which also harbored some very dangerous doctrines, he tried to withdraw. He wrote about this intention to several brethren and these letters are still in existence, but they would not hear of it. At that point Mozart's suffering began. He was abandoned by his former friends, died in bitter want, and was buried without attention."

There are a great many tales about Mozart's bad treatment at the hands of Masons, and it was even conjectured that they caused his death. Such stories probably became established because Masonric secrecy naturally intrigued simple-minded individuals. And the enemies of Freemasonry repeat them as if they were verified historical fact. We have already described the outpourings of Mathilde Ludendorff, but General Ludendorff himself also insisted in a polemic which appeared in 1926 on the anniversary of the battle of Lüttich that the Freemasons poisoned Mozart. Quoting from the ritual of the Grand Lodge of Germany, he proposed to annihilate Masonry by uncovering its secrets. He concluded:

"The secret of Masonry is the Jew. Freemasonry has undertaken to rob the German people of their Germanic pride, and to turn them, unawares, into an instrument for bringing about the glorious future of the Jewish people." He continued, "One generally assumes that the *Magic Flute* was written by Mozart in order to glorify Freemasonry. But he threaded an anti-Masonic legend into its web and that is the reason he was poisoned. In order to divert suspicion, the lodge asked him to compose a cantata. Another act of brotherly love caused his hands and feet to swell and caused vomiting. He died a few days later, in 1791, on the Day of Jehovah. Mozart had often voiced the suspicion that he was being poisoned, and when he was asked to compose the *Requiem,* he knew that the verdict of the lodge was about to be carried out."

Hermann Cohen takes a different view in his book, *Die dramatische Idee in Mozarts Operntexten* (Berlin, 1915). He is convinced that Mozart was a sincere Mason and wished to create a Masonic allegory. He summarizes his opinion: "The ethical ideal, brotherhood of men, and real, political peace on earth, this is the meaning of the *Magic Flute.* The Queen of the Night is the embodiment of a mother's tragedy." Here the inversion of the Masonic password concerning the incarnation of the son is relevant.

We point out that the conflict between mother and daughter properly belongs to the "dark" side of the story, while Tamino's initiation, the re-incorporation, the acceptance of the son Tamino by the father Sarastro, belongs to the "light" side. As in the fairy tale, the source of the opera, love, sublimated sexual love, is the prize of victory and virtue, the consummation of the ethical ideal. Hans Merian, in his book, *Mozarts Meisteropern* (Leipzig, 1900), goes beyond the Masonic interpretation. "The basic motif is the struggle between light and darkness, represented by Sarastro and the Queen of the Night. From Freemasonry Mozart has taken only the outward form of the ritual."

Arthur Schurig tries to reject all Masonic implications in his biography of Mozart. While Komorzynski already had doubts about a sudden change in the creation of the text, Schurig describes it as completely unified. According to him, the conflict between sacred and profane, as expressed in the opera, merely represents Mozart's own character. As an artist, the composer was well acquainted with heavenly spheres, but he also knew all-too-well the depths of this world.

In spite of all these attempts to minimize the Masonic influences in the *Magic Flute,* the most important scholars, such as Ludwig Schiedermair and Hermann Abert, were forced to admit that its uniqueness and its greatness are the result of Mozart's Masonry. Alfred Einstein intensively stressed the Masonic elements in the opera.

I should point out that in Masonic circles the Masonic interpretation has always been taken for granted. According to Grau-

PLATE 5.
Ignaz von Born, the "model of Sarastro."

PLATE 6.
Emanuel Schikaneder, librettist of the "Magic Flute."

penstein's history of the St. John's lodge in Hamburg, Brother Detenhoff gave a lecture, *Zufällige Gedanken über das Drama der Zauberflöte* (reflections on the drama of the *Magic Flute*) in the lodge "Pelikan" at Altona in 1794. This lecture is a counterpart of Batzko's allegory. For while Batzko did not fully realize the importance of Freemasonry in the opera, Detenhoff's lecture provides the first clear indication that it was completely understood by Masons. It anticipates Sonnleithner's interpretation by half a century. Detenhoff gives a rather detailed description of the text, calling Sarastro the personification of the "greatest and purest light," and the Queen of the Night, darkness which oppresses all mankind. He is struck by the fact that Papageno is punished as soon as he tells a lie. His punishment and reward, however, are on a strictly material level, which is all he wants. It would be impossible for such a gross person as Papageno to become a Mason. Tamino, on the other hand, aspires to higher things and finally gains admission to the temple.

THE MAGIC FLUTE: WORDS AND MUSIC

M ANY PASSAGES in the *Magic Flute* have either been taken directly from the Masonic ritual, or allude to it. For example, the *Sprecher* (orator) holds an important office in continental European lodges. In some countries, especially France, the orator occupies a high rank and is responsible for lodge discipline. The word "speaker" may have been taken directly from the novel, *Sethos.* The number three plays an important part in the *Magic Flute.* There are the three ladies, the three genii, finally the 18 (six times three) priests, which have a model in *Sethos.*

Quite possibly Schikaneder had read some other books on Egyptian Masonry too. C. W. Leadbeater discusses Egyptian Masonry in the ninth chapter of his book, *The Hidden Life in Freemasonry.* He describes a flaming star gleaming above the altar, and, indeed, the flaming star is depicted with the Masonic emblems on the title page of the original libretto. Also, according to Leadbeater, each brother brought to the ceremony his own light, a torch of pitchblende. These also appear in *Sethos,* as do the helmets that protect the warriors from the flames. Theatrical experts still refer to the Armored Men as firemen. We are reminded of the three genii by Leadbeater's description of two acolytes, a boy and a girl about twelve years old, chosen for their beauty and sworn to strictest secrecy. The hymn to Ra, the sun god, was important in the Egyptian ritual. Music and antiphonal choirs were also used.

Now for a detailed comparison of the Masonic ritual and the text of the libretto. In the first finale, upon entering the Masonic sphere, the genii sing:

> Such words are not for us to say
> Be silent, patient, persevering,
> A manly part thou hast to play
> If this the goal thou wouldst be nearing,

the three commandments given the Petitioner. Tamino replies:

What words do I read there inscribed on the gateway?
'To nature, to reason, to wisdom these temples.'

These are the three "Lesser Lights" of Freemasonry. In the next scene, a dialogue between Tamino and the priest contains a reference to the exclusion of women:

A woman then has told thee this?
'Twas like a woman thus to talk
And like a boy to think it true.

In the 22nd scene, Tamino sings:

Oh endless night, hast thou no breaking?
When dawns the day mine eyes are seeking?

This refers to the symbolic journey which is made blindfolded.

The scenes in front of the great temple are largely taken from *Sethos*. The stage setting is Egyptian. On each side there are nine pyramids, the tallest one in the middle. Sarastro informs the priests that Prince Tamino is waiting at the northern door for admission, with a virtuous heart, yearning for a state which can be attained only with great effort. Then Sarastro is asked three questions by the priests: "Is he virtuous? Can he be silent? Does he love his fellow-men?" These questions evidently refer to the part of the initiation which precedes the entrance of the initiate, the point at which his identity, reputation, etc., are asked. Sarastro's asking the priests whether they consider Tamino worthy of admission, and their signalling assent with gestures, also has a parallel with a portion of the Masonic initiation.

When the orator expresses doubt about Tamino's ability to stand up to his tests because of his royal blood, we are again reminded of *Sethos*, where the priests first receive the neophyte with doubt and disapproval. Sarastro's reply, "Still more, he is human," must have sounded quite revolutionary in the days of Emperor Leopold.

Then Tamino and his companion are led into the forecourt of the temple and the orator ("whom the gods through us appointed as defender of truth") is to teach them their duty to mankind. The orator exits with two priests, corresponding in the ritual to the exit of the Master, who then returns to the Petitioner.

In the third scene, the orator again asks the Prince whether he is prepared to risk his life in seeking his goal: "There is still time to turn back, but one more step and it will be too late." This warning has a parallel in the initiation, in which the Master points out to the initiate all the serious consequences of his entry into the Craft, admonishing him to return to worldly living if he cannot gather the strength. The warning to secrecy and silence is also found in the Masonic initiation.

The duet between orator and priests again refers to the exclusion of women:

> Beware the wiles of women's weaving,
> Would ye be worthy of this place.

Now follow the Prince's symbolic journey, the tests by fire and water, which are found in *Sethos* as well as in the Masonic initiation. And the final chorus of the priests again points to the three "Lesser Lights" (Strength, Beauty and Wisdom):

> Thanks to the great Osiris, thanks, Isis, to thee
> Through darkness and error they once sought their way,
> Victorious we hail them in triumph today.
> By nature directed, by reason protected,
> The high place of wisdom they now have found.

Even the serpent is a symbol well-known to Masonry, though not specifically part of its ritual. Abert guesses that it is a Masonic symbol of evil, and that before the Masonic slant was introduced it had been a fierce lion. But in Masonry, the serpent is related to the chain, a symbol of brotherhood. It is possible to interpret the serpent, which, after all, is killed by the "evil" three ladies, as a symbol of Masonry which is at first misunderstood by the uninitiated Tamino. In the earliest pictorial records of the *Magic Flute* the serpent, once killed, appears divided into three parts.

* * * * *

It has often been said that at least some parts of the *Magic Flute* were composed in a completely new style, so unique that it has been called the *Magic Flute*-style. The question is whether the deep humanitarian feeling gives the music its characteristic sound, or whether it was the specifically Masonic spirit which penetrated even the technical aspect of composition.

This style is present from the beginning of the opera on. The overture begins with three detached chords in E flat major, the key Mozart used to characterize solemnity. These chords represent the three knocks on the door; when they reappear in the middle of the overture they are a stylized version of the Entered Apprentice's knocking:　♫　Throughout the opera we find dotted rhythms. The three inversions of the triad have been combined with the Masonic rhythm, and the number three plays an important part.

The overture, particularly, reflects Masonic thinking. Its fugato theme, with pounding rhythms, has often been said to depict working on "the rough stone." To be sure, it is derived from a piano sonata by Clementi which Mozart had heard as a child at the court of Vienna. The first part presumably describes the first test. After enormous tension, caused by the peculiar, mysterious three-fold crescendo, it is concluded with the ceremonial chords of the winds. The development is a dark, unhappy sounding section, dwelling in minor and subdominant, probably representative of the self-examination. Note also the dialogue between winds and strings. Towards the end, the overture returns to the energetic E flat major and, after a recapitulation, it concludes with a ritual knocking signifying deliverance and redemption.

The march of the priests is genuine ritual music, with deceptive cadences and parallel sixths. Again, the three-fold sequence of eighth-note phrases. In order to properly appreciate the priests' scenes one must remember the fundamentally responsorial character of the ritual. In Sarastro's aria, "Oh hear us, Isis and Osiris," the atmosphere of mystery is achieved by the responses of the priests, signifying secrecy and ceremony.

In the first finale, the point at which the opera begins diverging from its original course, we at once feel the solemn atmosphere as the trumpets underscore the three-fold admonition, "Be silent, patient, persevering." But the Masonic mood has already been evident in the first trio of the three ladies.

Alfred Heuss was the first to write about the concept of humanitarian music in his article, *Die Humanitätsmelodien im Fidelio* (the humanitarian melodies in *Fidelio*), in *Zeitschrift für Musik*, vol. 91, no. 10. He characterizes it as having "a wonderful mildness and purity, silently glowing with metaphysical warmth," and shows that Beethoven was already composing such melodies before the *Magic Flute*. On the other hand, we find that these traits are already present in parts of *König Thamos* in the wonderfully sym-

91

metrical and solemn melodies which express man's harmonious relationship to the world and to man. It shows the traits which distinguished the classical man, severity with himself, tolerance of his fellows, and the desire to mold his own fate, in other words, a firm, integrated personality.

But the special quality of the *Magic Flute* is a sense of the mysterious, which appears in the first finale and recurs whenever the music expresses the mysteries of the initiates. For example, Tamino's question, "When wilt thou break the bond of silence?" and the orator's reply, "When friendship leads thee by the hand to join the temple's holy band." In this passage, the basses are parallel to the voices, while the strings pulsate softly, but the effect cannot be explained by technical means alone. When Tamino asks, later, "Oh, endless night, hast thou no breaking? When dawns the day mine eyes are seeking?" and the voices answer from within, "Soon, soon, or never!" we feel something of the enormous mystical power which Freemasonry held over Mozart.

The priests' march, "All hail to Sarastro," is more conventional, possibly because Papageno, the embodiment of worldliness, appears at that moment. The priests' march at the beginning of the second act, on the other hand, is strictly Masonic. The deceptive cadences, and later, the mysterious ascending parallel sixths eventually develop into a typical humanitarian melody. The introduction to the aria "Oh hear us, Isis and Osiris" again has these characteristic parallel sixths. Sarastro's aria, with its wide bass intervals, is also typical of Mozart's humanitarian melodies, expressing "wisdom, beauty, and strength."

The descending parallel sixths also appear in the priests' chorus, "Oh Isis and Osiris." Here they are probably indicative of the impressions which Mozart received as a child when he heard the Improperia by Palestrina or the fauxbourdon passages in Allegri's *Miserere* at St. Peter's Cathedral.

The most impressive part of the *Magic Flute* is, without doubt, the trial by fire. The beating rhythms, the imitative treatment, the sobbing of the violins, and the chromaticism elevate this section above the rest of the opera. The Armored Men sing a chorale which bears resemblance to a Protestant chorale, *Ach Gott im Himmel, sieh darein,* a resemblance with Masonic significance.

But the *Magic Flute* also gives artistic expression to some primordial elements in human culture. Initiation rites, such as trials by fire and water, are common to primitive peoples. The theme of death and resurrection is encountered in thousands of different forms in many cultures. The puberty rites of primitives were paralleled in higher civilizations by the association of men of similar outlook which, ultimately, led to Freemasonry. Some writers have interpreted this as a sign of the change from a matriarchal to a patriarchal society, while others see in it a protest by men against the rule of women (See Blüher, *Die Rolle der Erotik in der männlichen Gesellschaft*). Mastering the power over fire was just as important an idea in the mind of primitive man as birth from water.[1]

It is evident, then, that the fairy tale, the *Magic Flute,* had such an impact on some of the world's great minds because they realized, perhaps in a nebulous way, that it deals with some of man's oldest and deepest concepts. The libretto, in spite of its rather clumsy verses, is a book of human wisdom, consummated as a work of art by Mozart.

THE MAGIC FLUTE: SEQUELS

As WE HAVE ALREADY STATED, it took considerable time for the *Magic Flute's* relationships to Masonry to be generally acknowledged, and even today some scholars remain unconvinced. But the Masonic interpretation is strengthened by the fact that all of the various sequels contain Masonic elements. Evidently the Masonic significance of this opera was recognized from the very beginning at least by Masons.

We owe Goethe's fragment, *The Magic Flute, Part II,* to a performance of the opera in Weimar on January 16, 1794. Komorzynski has pointed out that Schikaneder was scorned by his contemporaries. We know that the literary classicists were hostile to him. Accordingly, his text was not used in the Weimar performance, but a new version was written by Christian August Vulpius, author of *Rinaldo* and Goethe's brother-in-law. The Vulpius version was published in Weimar and has appeared as a private printing for the *Gesellschaft der Bibliophilen.* Goethe thought very highly of Vulpius as a librettist, but in preferring his adaptation to the original, the prince of poets can safely be accused of having missed the boat. If Schikaneder's libretto is in places trivial, Vulpius's is full of banality. He changed a number of words, taking no account of the music, and thus caused the musical stresses to fall on the wrong words or syllables. He arbitrarily replaced the serpent by a dragon. This incident does not cast a favorable light on Goethe as a musician.

Let us show a few samples of the errors in accentuation which resulted from Vulpius's word changes. Obviously, the quotations must be in the original German. In the first scene, Tamino begins:

> *Zu Hülfe, zu Hülfe, er wird mich verschlingen,*
> *Wer hilft mir den giftigen Drachen bezwingen?*
> *Wie bin ich ermattet vom schrecklichen Kampf,*
> *O welch ein Qualm, o welch ein Dampf!*

94

Vulpius substituted this fourth line for
Ach rettet mich, ach schützet mich,

causing the word *welch* to be stressed by the music and thus violating the laws of German stress patterns. In the same number, the three ladies sing, with correct accentuation,
So schoen als ich noch nie gesehen.

But Vulpius makes them sing, with wrong stresses,
Wo kann man einen schönern sehen!

The substitution for
Wollt ich mein Herz der Liebe weih'n
dem schönen Jüngling sollt es seyn,
sounds like a parody or satire.

There are other points of disturbance. Instead of singing
Vielleicht, dass dieser schöne Mann
die vor'ge Ruh ihr geben kann,

the three ladies speak of a message,
auf die sie längst harrt, wie ihr wisst,
dass jetzt der Prinz gekommen ist.

Almost every line contains improper and disturbing changes of this sort.

Apparently Goethe was not satisfied with Vulpius's adaptation. He admits that "the well-known first part was full of improbabilities and jokes which few might understand and appreciate. But we have to admit that the author knew how to use contrasts to produce great dramatic effects."

This statement indicates that Goethe recognized the Masonic meaning of the *Magic Flute*. Indeed, he was a Mason himself and belonged to the lodge "Amalia" in Weimar. But he did not participate enthusiastically or fully. Nevertheless, Masonic thought was close to him, and the symbols of the Craft were his inspiration. When he wanted a musical setting for his sequel, he turned to a Masonic musician, Paul Wranitzky, whom we have met before.

The stage settings and costumes of the original *Magic Flute* were to be used in Goethe's sequel, so that continuity would be preserved. He already made some notes on the staging when he saw Vulpius's production. In 1803, Goethe asked Zelter to compose the music for this sequel, but it was not until 1814 that anything was done about it. Anselm Weber was also going to set it to music but completed only a few pieces.

This is the content of Goethe's sequel. Monostatos returns to the Queen of the Night with a group of Negroes in order to collect his reward for fulfilling a mission. He had been sent to take their newborn child from Tamino and Pamina and to place it in a golden coffin. "Have I been avenged," asks the queen, and the chorus replies, "Yes, Queen, you have." But the queen is not satisfied. The child is not in her possession because, when Monostatos started to carry the coffin to her, it became heavier and heavier, pulling its bearers to the ground. There it stayed and could not be moved. "Surely this is Sarastro's magic." But Monostatos had quickly locked the coffin with the queen's seal so that the child would remain imprisoned forever. The coffin is taken to the "Brotherly Order" which "learns and teaches wisdom in silent contemplation." But so great is the queen's power that, on being cursed by her, Tamino and Pamina would become insane if they were to see each other. If they laid eyes on their son, he would die. In the next scene, a procession of women carry the child's coffin. He is not allowed to rest so that he will not die. When they see Tamino, they retreat before him so that he cannot see his son. While Pamina and Tamino mourn their tragic loss, their misfortune is paralleled by Papageno's, who is dissatisfied with Papagena because she has not borne him any children. An invisible choir promises them that their wish will soon be fulfilled.

In the next scene, the priests are assembled in the temple. The orator says, "Before the northern door of our holy abode stands our brother, who has returned from a year's pilgrimage and seeks readmission." As a sign that he is still worthy of admission, the pilgrim brings a crystal ball enclosed in a silver band. It is now Sarastro's turn to wander for a year, and he does not hesitate to fulfill this command of the gods. His address is patterned after the aria in the *Magic Flute,* for he says, "Within these silent walls man finds himself and his innermost soul." (In the Vulpius version, he sang "Within these sacred walls.")

Of the following scenes, we have only sketches and rough drafts, for Goethe never completed them. Pamina wants to dedicate the golden casket to the sun, but the altar disappears into the ground before her eyes. On his wanderings Sarastro has encountered Papageno and Papagena. They tell him that they have found large, beautiful eggs in their hut and that they expect very beautiful birds to emerge from them. Sarastro advises them to put these eggs in a nest and cover them with flowers. Soon the eggs begin to swell up, and when they finally burst open, three children emerge from them, two boys and a girl ("musical and poetic jests"). Papageno now sings a song, *Von allen schönen Waren* (of all beautiful wares), which has been set to music by several composers. Among them is the Prague composer, Tomaschek, who begins the song with a fanfare-like introduction similar to the street-cries of old Prague, to the way the antique dealers of his time advertised their wares.

After the disappearance of the casket, Pamina searches for her husband, but when she sets eyes on him, both fall into a deep sleep. Thus the Queen of the Night has made good her threat. Papageno comes to the court and manages to alleviate their pain with his flute playing. Then some priests arrive with the news that the child lies in a deep cave, surrounded by water and fire.

In the second act, the parents penetrate this cave in order to save their child. Again, trials by water and fire. The Queen of the Night appears, attempting to keep the parents away. Suddenly the coffin opens and, while the guards throw their spears after it, the child flies away.

Of the rest of the opera only the scenario survived. The course of action is not clear, and Junk offers several theories. Presumably Sarastro has something to do with Papageno's children as part of his pilgrimage. Junk thinks that the children and Sarastro somehow save Tamino's child and restore it to its parents, and this concludes the high priest's function.

The role of Monostatos is also vague. It is likely that he tried to prevent the reunion of the child and its parents, which only Sarastro's power could bring about. The child is now in the hands of the Queen of the Night, and possibly Sarastro was to intervene at this point. Perhaps the issue is decided by a great battle from which Tamino emerges victorious. Curiously enough, the last remark in the scenario is "the vanquished priests." This would seem to indicate a victory of the forces of darkness, but that is impossible since the structure of the drama, and especially the tests, aim toward a happy ending. But we shall never discover with certainty what Goethe intended.

Again, I should like to discuss the Masonic features of Goethe's fragment. There are, above all, the trial scenes. In the first part, Pamina and Tamino undergo these tests in order to become man and wife, and in the second part, to be united with their child. But while Schikaneder arranged them in the order of abstinence, trial by fire, and trial by water, Goethe reverses them. In his fragment, the fire and water trials are followed by the spiritual test, symbolized by separation from the child. Junk points out that Goethe chose the only logical order, namely, first the physical tests, then the spiritual. But we must be aware that the trials by fire and water are purely symbolic and that a distinction between spiritual and physical tests is irrelevant.

It is also possible that Goethe intentionally contradicted Masonic symbolism, for he accepted the Masonic ritual only with reservations.[1] The priest's journey (Sarastro is chosen by lot), on the other hand, may be a protest of Goethe against Masonic practices. He wants real pilgrimages, not only symbolic ones, deeds in addition to words. In this respect Goethe's thinking places him among modern Masons of the activist persuasion. When Sarastro says, "Within these silent walls man finds himself and his innermost soul," he probably refers to the ceremony in the "dark chamber."

It would be interesting to know whether Goethe's second part of the *Magic Flute* was in any way influenced by Schikaneder's-P. v. Winter's own sequel, *Das Labyrinth oder der Kampf mit den Elementen* (the labyrinth or the fight with the elements), published in 1792. The piano arrangement bears no date and shows a title different from that given by Komorzynski. The engraving on the title page depicts three split columns in a landscape of woods and lakes.

Schikaneder's characters from the *Magic Flute* have remained, and some new ones have been added. Monostatos now has a companion, the Negress Gura. Papageno has found parents and siblings. Typheus and Sithos are new representatives of the realm of darkness.

The overture begins with the three chords we know so well from the *Magic Flute*, but in C major and without change of inversion. It is written in the conventional, rather playful style of Singspiel, but there is an attempt to portray the forces of darkness in the introduction by sequences of seventh chords and slurs in the double basses.

In the prologue, we first see the Queen of the Night and her three female attendants, whose speech is similar in style to that of the *Magic Flute*. The three ladies offer Tamino and Pamina a poisonous drink. They are foiled by Sarastro's warning voice, which joins in the ensemble. In a finale, the couple are proclaimed king and queen. The Queen of the Night sings a recitative aria modeled on Mozart's revenge aria, announcing the arrival of the great Typheus who has come to avenge her: *Bald naht sich die Stunde zu verderben diese Brut* (the hour is near for destroying this rabble). Papageno's scenes are in the Neapolitan style with a popular Viennese flavor. Typheus and Sithos now appear and, in the name of the Queen of the Night, demand Pamina. The priests prepare for battle while a chorus of the forces of darkness challenges them and threatens their annihilation.

The lovers must now undergo yet another test, the walk through a labyrinth. Sarastro's aria, *Nun wandelt ruhig eure Strasse* ("Now walk your path with confidence") is again reminiscent of Mozart's style. Tamino is given the flute, while Pamina is to wear a veil, a sign of her virtue, which she must always protect. During the journey she is seized by four Negroes and taken into the realm of darkness. Papageno, also parted from his wife, captures Monostatos in a woods and the three ladies, who try to flatter him into giving them his glockenspiel, are made to dance until they drop.

Finally, Papageno rescues Pamina and takes her to the initiates. Leaping through the air, she joins Tamino and hand in hand, accompanied by flutes and the march rhythms of kettledrums, they successfully undergo their trial. The forces of darkness take up pursuit and a pitched battle follows. Finally, Typheus is pushed over a precipice into a raging fire, Monostatos is chained to a rock, and the power of the Queen of the Night is broken forever. The final chorus assures us:

> To eternal punishment, eternal damnation
> Isis has condemned the powers of darkness.
> Fettered in eternal chains by virtue,
> The Queen of the Night will harm us no more.
> Virtue has finally trodden her in dust,
> Has freed herself from the burden of sin.

It is difficult to decide to what extent Goethe's sequel is related to Schikaneder's. There are a great number of similarities, such as the children of Papageno, the role of Monostatos, the repetition of the tests; all these point to some kind of relationship.

In any case, the Masonic influences in Schikaneder's second part are very much less noticeable than in the *Magic Flute*. Freemasonry was not a timely subject in Austria after the death of Joseph II. Moreover, Schikaneder had been suspended from the Craft with dishonor, and the composer, Winter, was not a Mason. Even so, the music has some Masonic elements, the knocking rhythmic effects and three-fold repetitions, for example.

And so we see that the *Magic Flute* cast its influence about in many ways. It is noteworthy that two men of greatly differing caliber, Goethe and Schikaneder, occupied themselves with the same problem. But while for Goethe the material was too rich, Schikaneder was able to whip up yet another opera with the greatest of ease.

The impact of the *Magic Flute* on Goethe can be seen from its traces in his "Tale." We find it not only in the renunciation motif, but also in a scene in a subterranean temple. Quite clearly these are patterned after scenes in the *Magic Flute,* which had just been performed at Weimar. The old man proclaims, "There are three things which rule here on earth: wisdom, beauty, and strength." Goethe imposed a fourth power above these, love.

A series of sequels to the *Magic Flute* also appeared during the 19th century. In connection with Goethe's fragment, I should like to mention one by Wilhelm Rintel, the son of Zelter's daughter, Adelheid, and Dr. Ludwig Wilhelm Rintel. A musician without stature, this composer of the *Magic Flute, Part II* died in Berlin in 1899. In his memoirs he wrote that he had intended to realize a plan close to his grandfather's heart. From the exact contents of this opera, compiled by Georg Richard Kruse, we see that very little of Goethe's fragment actually survived in it.

Yet another sequel comes from the pen of Heinrich August Schulze, whose libretto, *Nitokris, der Zauberflöte 2. Teil, Oper in drei Akten im Anschluss an Schikaneder-Mozart, und mit Anlehnung an Goethes Fragment von Dr. Martin Schulze* ("Nitokris, part II of the Magic Flute, in three acts, being a sequel to the opera by Schikaneder-Mozart, and based on the fragment by Goethe, by Dr. Martin Schulze") was published in Darmstadt in 1886. The libretto was written by the composer's son. I conclude

100

this list by mentioning *Zarastro* by Göpfert, which typifies the poor quality of all these sequels and completions of Goethe's fragment. For as the satellites revolve around their sun, only to disintegrate, these various imitations of the *Magic Flute* have sunk into oblivion. Only Mozart's masterpiece is truly immortal and symbolic of humanity. A chapter devoted to it can properly be closed with the lines of Hermann Hesse, who has expressed in poetry what I, and many before me, have tried to say in prose.

> Then I shall hear you once again today,
> Beloved music, and shall be a guest
> In light's great temple, with its choirs of priests,
> And listen to the sounds of flutes divine.
> So many times, throughout these passing years
> Have I looked forward to this wondrous play
> And each time did renew the ancient vow
> Which joins me to you in the chain of men
> United in the journey to the sun;
> Each time I marveled that this brotherhood
> Which has no home, no land to call its own,
> Continues to command a million souls
> Desiring labor in its secret ranks.
> But this reunion strikes a hidden fear.
> Tamino, will my old and tired ear,
> My weary heart and mind, will they again
> Be worthy of the greatness of your sounds,
> Or will they fail to grasp your message now?
> Eternal youth is yours, you blessed spirits.
> Oblivious to the ups and downs of nations
> You will remain our brothers, leaders, masters,
> Until from our dead hands the torch must tumble.
> But when some day your hour has struck, and men
> Will fail to recognize your brotherhood,
> New signs will rise upon the firmament
> To take the place of yours, for all mankind
> Has need of inspiration such as this.

MOZART'S LIFE

How important was Freemasonry in Mozart's life? This is the question we now turn to. The comparatively short time (1784-1791) during which he belonged to the Craft was one of great productivity. To these years belong his most important compositions: *The Marriage of Figaro, Don Giovanni, Cosi fan tutte,* his greatest symphonies and chamber music. An examination of Mozart's whole life, with reference to Masonry, may show the importance of the Craft in a new light.

Born in Salzburg in 1756, Mozart was a child prodigy. His musical talent was soon universally recognized and in 1761, when he was only five and a half, he gave his first public performance in the *Aula* of the university. One year later, his performances were of such caliber that the proud father took Wolfgang and his eleven-year-old sister on a tour to Munich and Vienna. Soon they went to Paris, stopping at various courts in Bavaria, Württemberg, and the Palatinate. At seven, Mozart gave a concert in Frankfurt, an event which Goethe remembered years later. Concerts followed in Coblenz, Trier, and Aachen, before the stern Princess Amalia of Prussia, the sister of Frederick the Great. After stopping in Brussels, the family reached Paris on Nov. 18, 1763. They found a sponsor in Baron Melchior Grimm, who is famous for his protests against the artificiality of French opera. They performed for Madame Pompadour, before the king and queen, and, with royal permission, gave two public concerts. Mozart's first two published compositions appeared in Paris.

From Paris they went to London, performing before the royal family and Johann Christian Bach, the queen's conductor. From London to the Hague, but in Lille, Wolfgang and his sister became critically ill. Then the journey continued to Paris, Dijon, Bern, Zürich, Donaueschingen, Ulm, and Munich. They returned to Salzburg in 1766, after an absence of three years.

Now Mozart wrote his first oratorio, *Die Schuldigkeit des*

ersten Gebotes. After barely one year of serious study, the family again took the road to Vienna. Driven to Olmütz by an epidemic of smallpox, they returned to Vienna as soon as they had recovered. There they performed before Joseph II, who commissioned the opera *La Finta Semplice.* The producer Afflisio accepted it but various intrigues prevented its performance. But *Bastien et Bastienne* fared better, and Mozart, then twelve years old, conducted the premiere, together with a mass for the consecration of the *Waisenhauskirche.*

The following year, Mozart was made concert master to the Archbishop of Salzburg and immediately went to Italy with his father. According to Leopold's reports, this journey turned into a triumphal procession. The churches and theaters where he performed were filled to overflowing. He acquitted himself brilliantly in the difficult examinations given him by Sammartini in Milan and Padre Martini in Bologna. The court at Naples was delighted with him, and in Rome he was made a Cavalier of the Order of the Golden Spur. In Bologna he was appointed a member of the *Accademia filarmonica.* At Milan, then, the Mozarts stopped for a longer period; the opera *Mitridate* had its first performance at Christmas, 1770, and was successfully given twenty times. Father and son returned to Salzburg in the Spring of 1771, but by Fall they were back in Milan.

All these journeys were made possible by the benevolence of Archbishop Schrattenbach, who evidently recognized Wolfgang's genius and did not object to these projects. But his successor, Hieronymus von Colloredo, was a dull and basically unartistic individual who did not approve. At Christmas, 1772, Mozart was again in Milan for the performance of his opera *Lucio Silla.* He composed, conducted, and gave concerts in many places, always with outstanding success, but he still had no regular suitable employment. His father was planning another concert tour, but the archbishop refused him leave and Mozart felt obliged to resign in order to try his luck elsewhere.

This time Wolfgang traveled with his mother. They went to Munich, Augsburg, and Mannheim, where Mozart fell in love with the singer Aloisia Weber, and finally to Paris. His mother's death in 1778 was a great loss. Famous without really having achieved anything, he returned to Salzburg and again entered the archbishop's service. In 1779 he was made court organist. *Ido-*

meneo, the transition to his great classical works, was written for Munich.

Meanwhile Mozart's relations to the archbishop had become increasingly strained, until he finally left Salzburg and settled in Vienna. But there he also found no regular employment, though the emperor commissioned *Die Entführung aus dem Serail.* In 1782 he married Constanze Weber, but his marriage brought him only more financial difficulties. In 1786, *Figaro* was performed, and, in 1787, that opera of operas, *Don Giovanni.* In 1789, urged and accompanied by Prince Karl Lichnowsky, he went to Berlin, giving concerts in Dresden, Leipzig, and before Frederick William II in Potsdam. *Cosi fan tutte* appeared the next year and, in the last year of his life, *La Clemenza di Tito,* composed for the coronation of Leopold II in Prague, and his swansong, the *Magic Flute.* The *Requiem,* surrounded by legends, was his last work.

Let us contemplate this life of Mozart's, with its unrest, its constant pursuit of success under the tyranny of his father; its incredible wealth of acquaintances, its numerous successes and failures, its strains and its times of depression; this kaleidoscope of an artist's life of adventure, beginning in its early days under the strict and single-minded guidance of the father who wanted nothing so much as his son's success. And with all this, the overwhelming desire to create, the wealth of musical visions which never allowed him a moment's rest, and which must be committed to paper.

Let us also consider the musical environment in which Mozart was placed: Salzburg, a stuffy provincial town dominated by the archepiscopal court with its narrow conception of art; in contrast, the infinite variety of impressions on his long journeys. In the large towns of Germany he heard Italian opera, which greatly impressed him when he was still a child. In London he became acquainted with the music of Christian Bach, in Paris with French opera and instrumental music in the ferment of preclassical "storm and stress." From Bohemia and Mannheim came a new, affected style of symphonic music. Later, in Vienna, again a different, conservative mode of musical thinking, juxtaposed to Gluck's operatic reforms. Then, in Italy, Wolfgang assimilated the essentials of Italian opera to such a degree that he almost became the *maestro italianissimo.* The impressions gained from Italian chamber music were almost as strong as the later ones from Haydn. In

Salzburg and Vienna, the fashionable German *Singspiel* constituted yet another influence on his style. There is not enough space to enumerate the manifold musical impressions Mozart must have received in the course of his life.

It would appear that Mozart's decision finally to settle in Vienna was the artistic synthesis of all these musical styles and influences. His many trials and privations, human and artistic, led to the integration of his character and music. It is noteworthy that in this period of integration, 1782-1785, he showed great interest in the older style of Handel and Bach, a style also reflected in his Masonic compositions. Of the utmost importance was his rejection of the affected "storm and stress" style, because, instead, he created the new classical style. All this is concentrated in the period immediately preceding his initiation into Freemasonry. Neither orthodox Catholicism nor the new rationalism succeeded in satisfying him. What led him to Masonry was the reflection and self-contemplation which followed his extensive wandering, and this also brought about the creation of his unique style. This is the meaning of Mozart's entry into the Craft. It is the coronation of the master, and we are safe in saying that the part of Freemasonry in his life was so decisive that the degree of its contribution to art has been grossly underestimated.

MOZART THE MAN

IT IS A TRUISM that only a good man can be a good Mason. If Mozart had never joined a lodge, we still might think of him as a Mason without insignia. Nature had given him a high sense of ethics, and the excellent education which he received was equally designed to prepare him for his musical career and to make of him a man of refinement and culture and moral integrity. His father, Leopold Mozart, was of Swabian stock, and the Swabs are reputed to combine in their character the opposites of stubbornness and sensibility, of reticence and cordiality, of sober thought and dreamy brooding. Indeed, Leopold's character encompasses all these polar pairs. In him the highest artistic endeavor alternates with practical sobriety, rationalism with a profound sense of religion, Catholic dogma with Masonic ideals. His perseverance in the pursuit of a goal once set is a trait which Leopold handed down to his son, and the same holds true for his inflexible sense of duty and his painstaking conscientiousness. Leopold Mozart—like Goethe and Byron—belongs to that numerous clan of major and minor adventurous souls whose "storming and stressful" romantic impulse induced them to look for salvation or for success in distant lands on distant shores, at the courts of great nations, or in the palaces of the mighty. Wolfgang's innate imagination received the richest nourishment during the trips of his very early childhood. Yet these same trips—and this we must say, though it may well be construed as a reproach leveled at Leopold—contributed doubtless through the physical hardship they involved to the undermining of Mozart's health and hence to his early death. Leopold Mozart was a wonderful manager of his son's education, and yet, the rationalist in him cannot be spared the reproach that in exploiting his precious possession of a child prodigy he was not free from selfish motives. Leopold was recognized by his family as an unchallenged authority. "Right after God comes Papa." The decrees of this authority Wolfgang heeded up to the point where he felt that he had to make his way through life by himself, without regard for the laws of his father, in full subservience to no master but his inner self and his genius. This came to pass about the year 1781 when he turned his back on Archbishop Colloredo, left the stuffy atmosphere of his native Salzburg, and settled for good in Vienna. This, then, was the time when he resisted his father's will with both energy and success and made Konstanze Weber his wife, incurring thereby Leopold's greatest displeasure. In these matters Mozart was a representative of modern times, both as a man and as an artist. And it is characteristic of him and of the spirit of his times that his years at Vienna, when he suffered the misery and the heartache of a misunderstood genius, were in creative terms the richest years of his life.

Mozart's mother hailed from a family that can be traced in the region of Salzburg to her grandfather Bartholomäus Pertl, identified as an archepiscopal coachman. She was born on Christmas day 1720 at St. Gilgen near Salzburg where the *Pflegerhaus*— i.e. the residence of the county prefect—on the lovely shores of Lake Wolfgang is still to be seen in our days. She was given the Christian names of Anna Maria. About the year 1770, the painter Pietro Antonio Lorenzoni made a portrait of her: A beautiful and portly woman with an expression of charm and dignity who evidently deserved her share in the contemporary verdict that the Mozarts—Leopold and his wife—were Salzburg's most handsome married couple. Many traits in her son's character were inherited from her. Her role in the family was not an easy one, for time and again she had to mediate between the hard-headed stubbornness of her husband and the playful abandon of her children who did not always mind if one of their father-decreed duties remained unattended to. She was a paragon of tact and kindness and literally sacrificed her life for her son when in the summer of 1778 in Paris, far away from her loved ones, she succumbed to a treacherous illness. If she had not insisted on accompanying her son on his second trip west, she doubtless would have been saved to act for a long time to come her part of the family's warden of mediation. There can be no doubt that she would have succeeded in forestalling the conflict between Leopold and Wolfgang.

It would be wrong to assume that the discord between father and son was solely due to Wolfgang's marriage. The trouble had been smoldering since the summer of 1778, that is, since the tragic hours of Anna Maria's death at Paris. We need not go so far as to suppose that Leopold held his son responsible for the death of his deeply beloved wife, although it is true that many of his letters to his son express the bitterness of his feelings in the face of so dreadful a loss. The true reason for the split lies deeper. It has its roots in the very nature of Wolfgang. Leopold had been an excellent drillmaster of the boy prodigy, and now he could not and would not understand that his son—a divinely inspired genius —had to follow the law of his own personality. When Wolfgang matured into the ranks of the masters, Leopold stood by helpless and uncomprehending. He could not get, nor get over it, that his son—the very son whose every step had been of his planning— should go and should have to go his own way. This lack of understanding on the part of Leopold is strikingly apparent from the exchange of letters between father and son at the time when Wolfgang severed the ties of his employment at Salzburg. On May 9, 1781, Wolfgang wrote: "I am still full of gall, and you, my best and dearest father, are doubtless so with me. My patience has been tried for so long. But finally it foundered anyway. I am no longer so unhappy as to be in the employ of Salzburg. . . . Beyond all this, I beg you to take heart, for now my luck begins, and I hope my luck will be yours too." The point at issue was the humiliating treatment which had been meted out to Mozart by Archbishop Colloredo and his major-domo, Count Arco, who actually had kicked him with his booted foot. Indeed, one is tempted to observe that in these happenings a symbol may be seen of the transition in the artist's social standing from the Baroque to modern times.

In the world of the Baroque, the musician is the servant of his master. He serves a prince, or he serves some other authority. His every product serves a specific purpose, and that purpose is dictated from without. Bach wrote his Cantatas and his Passions for the full cycle of the Christian year. This was his duty as stipulated in his contract of employment. It sounds paradoxical to us but it is true that such a genius as the Cantor of the Thomasschule at Leipzig had to indenture his creative powers to the demands of the times or the whims of an authority. His creative will is not free: when Christmas or Easter approaches, he must subject the flight of his fancy to the spirit and the mood of the occasion. He writes a cantata for the Epiphany, another for the Feast of the Reformation. His instrumental works are done at the behest of whoever happens to be his master at the time. They are written for the occasion, for this particular day. They are not written for eternity and do not spring from the deepest creative urge of the composer. The man of the Baroque does not live from within. He conceives of himself as an element in a pattern ordained by God. With modern man all this is radically different. He creates his own world in accordance with the autonomous decrees of his personality and often enough gathers his strength for a heroic struggle against fate. Beethoven is the classical example of this type of man: "We need to plant a fist onto the jaws of fate." ("Man muss dem Schicksal in den Rachen greifen.") Indeed, it is hard to think of a more striking exemplification of the artist's autonomy than Beethoven whose gigantic determination enabled him to take on illness, loss of hearing, and all the vicissitudes of his destiny and to create works of art that shall not perish from this earth in centuries untold. It seems impossible to picture Beethoven in a red musician's livery waiting servilely on Prince Lichnowsky or Prince Lobkowitz. When in 1806 Lichnowsky had Beethoven as his guest at his castle of Grätz near Troppau, he meant to entertain a group of French officers that were billeted on him by having the great musician play for them. Beethoven exploded. He told the prince in no uncertain terms what he thought of him, got himself whatever transportation happened to be available in those parts, and drove straight back to Vienna. Rumor has it that back in Vienna he smashed the prince's statue.

Yet the selfsame prince, years later, would stealthily tiptoe through Beethoven's rooms intent upon the blissful experience of watching the genius at work, while Beethoven would not deign to take note of his presence. Lobkowitz, we are told, did not fare much better when once he dared to make a critical remark about the performance of one of Beethoven's symphonies. When on his way home the composer passed the Lobkowitz residence, he shouted through the open door, "Lobkowitz, you are an ass!"

These two anecdotes are eminently suited to point up the change that had taken place in the sociology of art. No baroque composer would have dared harbor such revolutionary thoughts, let alone express them. Joseph Haydn occupies in these matters an intermediate position. He, too, was obliged to wear a red musician's livery when waiting upon his master, Count Morzin at Lukawetz, and later on, Prince Esterhazy at Eisenstadt. He too was obliged to produce compositions at the rate of about one a week. But in his case there was a "patriarchal" element in the relation of master and servant. Haydn's innate good nature and his healthy and, as it were, spontaneous servility made it easy for him to maintain the baroque combination of artist and servant. His removal to Vienna and his visits to democratic Britain, where the successes of his art accrued to a heretofore unheard-of triumph for him as a person, would seem to put him on a par, at least to a certain extent, with the composers of subsequent ages.

In Mozart's life the break with the baroque past was a more painful and violent process. To understand this we need but read the letter he wrote his father on March 17, 1781, from Vienna. The way he was being treated in Archbishop Colloredo's house-hold—the Archbishop was at the time in Vienna and had his Salzburg entourage join him—contrasts sharply with the honors which the young musician had been accorded on the occasion of the performance of *Idomeneo* at Munich: "At 12 o'clock noon, unfortunately a little early for me, we sit down and eat. The table is set for the 2 gentlemen and heart-and-soul chamber valets, the Honorable Comptroller [E. M. Kölnberger], Mr. Zetti [the Chamber Furrier], 2 cooks, Signor Cecharelli and Signor Brunetti, and little me. N.B. The 2 Privy Chamber Valets sit at the head of the table. I have at least the honor of being seated ahead of the cooks. The conversation at table consists of silly and rather coarse stories." It is not hard to understand that this Salzburg version of a treatment in the style of the ancien régime could not satisfy the young master who knew his worth and had become accustomed during his concert tours to being pampered by nobility and clergy. The height of his annoyance and the final break with the Arch-bishop are reflected in the famous passage of a letter he wrote in May, 1781. The Archbishop keeps pestering Mozart with the question as to when he is going to get back to Salzburg: " 'Well, fellow, when are you going to go?' I replied: 'I meant to go to-night, but all the seats were taken.'—Then he kept going in the same vein telling me I was the most dissolute person he knew and none of his people served him as badly as I; he advised me to leave this very day, otherwise he will write home that they should withhold my pay—it was impossible to squeeze in a word, it kept going like a brush fire. I listened calmly; he lied to my face I was getting 500 fl. pay, called me a good-for-nothing, a louse, a fop, I don't like to write it all down. Finally, when I was getting hot under the skin, I said: Your Princely Grace, are you not satisfied with me, Sir? What? Are you trying to threaten me? Oh, you fop. There is the door! Look, I won't have anything to do with such a miserable wretch.—Finally I said: Neither I with you.— Then go,—and I: while on my way out.—Let us keep it that way. Tomorrow you will get it in writing."

Mozart's break with the Archbishop is most intimately connected with his alienation from his father and in part also from his sister and with his increasing dislike of the whole stuffy atmosphere of Salzburg. In this break and this alienation we should see nothing less than the tangible expression of the ultimate liberation of Mozart's genius from the burden of duty and routine and from his years of bondage within and without. The child prodigy turns into a talent, and the talent in turn accomplishes the breakthrough to the unique status of a genius. We can imagine that all these vexations and all this disgust with Salzburg and its Archbishop contributed not a little to his decision toward the end of the year 1784 to accept Baron von Gemmingen's invitation to join the lodge "Zur Wohltätigkeit" ("Charity"). For there he found true friends: Noblemen, scientists, artists and writers, and other respected and respectable citizens who took him as a human being and treated him as a brother and who honored and appreciated him and his talent. He also met Haydn, his revered master, to whom he dedicated his six great quartets at just about this time. The text of the dedication was written in Italian. We reproduce it here in translation. It reads as follows: "When a father decides to let his children go out into the world, he thinks it wise to entrust their protection and guidance to a man of fame and thinks himself lucky when that man has been his best friend. So then, you famous man who are my dearest friend, take these six children of mine. They are the fruits of long and arduous work. Yet the hope, fostered by some friends, that I may see these labors rewarded at least in part, gives me courage and I indulge the flattering thought that these results of my creation will some day repay me with equal solace. You yourself, dear friend, have told me of your satisfaction at the time of your last sojourn in this capital. This applause from you is the prime stimulus which makes me entrust my children into your hands; it is the justification of my hope that they will not prove unworthy of your good graces. May you deign to accept them and be their procreator's guide and friend. From this moment I relinquish into your hands my rights in them but beg you to be lenient toward their flaws which the prejudice of paternal vision may have concealed from me and to preserve, with or without them, your friendship for him who thinks of them so highly. With all my heart, dear friend, I am your sincere friend W. A. Mozart." In this context it is essential to underline the personal relationship between Mozart and Haydn, for there is no doubt that the friendship of these two in the realm of music received a mighty boost through the community of their masonic experiences.

If we attempt to describe the man Mozart, we cannot help being struck by his physical appearance. His stature is by no means of a kind one would be apt to call imposing. He is often mistaken for some underling until the embarrassing discovery is made that this indifferent little man is the great master Mozart. One famous person once mistakes him for a journeyman artisan. At times Mozart accepts situations of this kind in good humor, but we must note that in regard to his external appearance he does have a kind of inferiority complex. An expression of this concern is his endeavor to dress well. Indeed, he goes rather too far in this and does not seem to mind making himself conspicuous at times. He certainly is vain, and he takes particular pride in the beauty of his hands. He is fond of lace and jewelry and reminds us in this respect of Richard Wagner whose transvestism is well known. Mozart's standard attire is a blue coat with tails and gold buttons, knee breeches, and shoes with silver buckles. When he has to conduct an orchestra, Konstanze must have his red tail coat ready which is the typical musician's uniform at Mozart's time as it had been at the time of Bach. Mozart's entire body is a bundle of nerves. His hands are always playing, as though all things in this world were pianos. His nervousness is an effect of the restless life he had to lead during his childhood when the stage coach was his home and the highways of Europe his country. His facial expression has nothing out of the ordinary. There is no trace of his genius in his physiognomy and nothing demoniac as in the case of Beethoven or E. T. A. Hoffmann or Paganini. But all this changes when he sits down at the piano and begins to improvise. Then, to use the expression coined by his biographer Niemetschek, "his eyes reposed grave and collected." A symbol of concentration! One of Mozart's most striking characteristics is his keen observation of human nature. His letters offer classical examples of psychological insight—a power which his artistic genius exploited in another realm in the form of his inspired dramatic characterizations. He is full of humor and wit and occasionally not adverse to crude pleasantries. The obscenities which occur in many of his letters (especially those addressed to the famous Bäsle) and in his canons, must be understood as part of the Salzburg atmosphere. In the Mozart household earthy stories and earthy words were not considered out of place, in keeping with the principle, "naturalia non sunt turpia." The "mot de Cambronne" which occurs so often in the canons was standard usage. Even the upper classes, the nobility and the princes, attributed no extraordinary importance to such matters, as may be seen in the letters of Elizabeth Charlotte, the Palatine princess who married the brother of Louis XIV. In Mozart's case these scurrilities have the additional psychological explanation that they afforded the master a kind of relaxation after his taxing work. Puns often with scarcely ambiguous implications were not beneath Beethoven either.

Mozart was not endowed with a settled character of purpose and determination as was Beethoven. His life was made harder by his good nature, an occasional lack of energy, a frequently recurring inclination to take it easy, and a baseless optimism. The keen observer of human nature, Baron Melchior de Grimm— the very same who had presented to the astonished Parisians and to the world the child prodigy as a miracle of nature but who apparently appreciated the mature artist less than the earlier miracle—wrote to Leopold from Paris under a dateline of 1778: "Wolfgang is too good-hearted, too weak, too gullible, and too inexperienced in the ways of success. If he had only half his talent but twice his skill, I would not worry about him." And Leopold adds the note: "All that is well taken." In two letters of Leopold's we find the same criticism in a more paternally direct wording: "There are two reasons that prevent you from using your intelligence as you should. Study yourself! Get to know yourself! —— You are too conceited, and you are too egotistical. And then that you are always so chummy right from the start and you open your heart to everybody." And yet, it is wrong to say, as Schurig did in his classical biography (II, 314), that Wolfgang was no man of action, no determined, tenacious, and relentless fighter but a dreamer and on most occasions a fatalist. The exact opposite is nearer the truth. He was a mighty worker, and what he accomplished during the last years of his life is a unique performance in the history of human endeavor. For just as Beethoven wrote his greatest works while fighting fate, while struggling against deafness and disease, so Mozart wrote his greatest works—*The Abduction, Figaro, Don Giovanni, The Magic Flute,* the *Requiem,* his great symphonies and his great chamber music—during the last ten years of great financial straits, when no one helped him, when his creditors pressed him and petty critics pestered him, when he was neglected and scorned and had to be a witness to fate's preferring innumerable nitwits and bunglers to him who was the greatest genius of his age. And indeed, these last ten years of Mozart's life, this long series of disappointments and insults with but a rare ray of light to relieve the cruel monotony of hardship, show him as the great fighter who consciously takes on the powers of destiny, even though his everyday demeanor may at times show him in a rather different light. That cannot be changed and will always remain a fact, even if a Nissen, his earliest biographer, reduces the great productivity of his final years to the simple explanation that he seemed to be so much busier because he wrote down more. For one thing is certain: Mozart's whole life was music. And writing down and working over his musical fantasies was precisely the work he had to carry through. The genius of Mozart was never inactive for as long as a second throughout his entire life. Even while bowling and at billiards the musical thoughts came flowing to him in unheard-of abundance, and we are told that he often managed to be at work on several compositions at once, exactly as this was the case with Beethoven.

This is the place to speak of Mozart's attitude toward the Church and religion as a faith and a dogma. It is but natural that the Mozart children were brought up in the faith of the Catholic atmosphere of the Court at Salzburg. It is also but natural that they felt themselves to be good Catholics. Leopold was of course a true son of the Church, although his religious ideas were strongly affected by the rationalistic trends of the age. Rationalism had managed to get a foothold even at the University of Salzburg. A critical observer like Leopold was bound to catch on to some heretical notions while watching the hypocrisies that were rampant at Salzburg. And some such notions he may well have passed on to his son. It goes without saying that Mozart's mother was Catholic in a less complicated and hence more thoroughgoing sense. It seems evident that so intricate a matter as the principle of the credo quia absurdum never as much as entered her head. In Wolfgang's case it is the psychology of his character that makes us understand that no faith could be as dear to him as the Catholic Faith. Only the Catholic form of worship with the breath-taking splendor of its festivities, its sensuous impressiveness, the Corpus Christi procession, the parish fairs and country-wakes, the May time services, Christmas crèches, and Easter festivities could meet the demands of his imagination. How could Mozart's glowing vision have endured the quiet and almost abstract atmosphere of Lutheranism or the puritanical dryness of the Calvinists? It may be objected that Bach's music was rooted in the Lutheran faith, but is it not true that his cantatas and masses and Passions sprang from the imaginative inspiration of the Bible, and did not his works draw richer nourishment from the Pietists' mystical broodings than from the orthodox principles of the dogma? What Mozart's thoughts were in his younger years can be inferred from the words he wrote on October 25, 1777: "I always see God before me. I recognize His omnipotence. I live in awe of His wrath. But I also know His love, His mercy, and His compassion. He will never abandon His servants. If His will is done, mine too is done, and nothing can go wrong." When we analyze this passage a little more carefully we are struck to see that he identifies his will with the will of God. That brings to mind the tenets of pantheism or again the thinking of Johannes Scheffler's Cherubinic Pilgrim, who said that he cannot live without God as God cannot live without him. We may call Mozart's religious feeling at this time a combination of Deism, Mysticism, and Pantheism which nonetheless had no trouble manifesting itself in the garb of Catholic appearances. In his letters to Leopold religious references grow ever rarer as time goes on. From time to time there are mordant remarks about the clergy, even before his masonic initiation. More and more frequently Leopold feels the need to inquire about his son's fasts, confession, and communion. As late as 1791, a few months before his death, Mozart informs his wife that he has taken part, candle in hand, in a Corpus Christi procession. But we must not overlook the fact that this report appears in a letter which Mozart signed with his fool's name, Snai. Considerable importance may attach to this point. Numerous works of Church music of Mozart's middle years bear witness to the profound mysticism of their creator. This impression is especially inescapable in those passages in the Masses which are concerned with Incarnation, Resurrection, and Redemption, such as "Tollis peccata mundi" and "Et incarnatus" and "Resurrexit." We may assume that the idea of resurrection—with which later on he became familiar in the different form of the Hiram legend—had occupied him from the time of his earliest youth. This is quite evident in a passage written in Paris and referring to the death of his mother: "Under those mournful circumstances I found solace in three ways, namely through my complete and implicit trust in God's will, then through the present memory of her unsuffering and beautiful death, by imagining how now in one moment she is to be happy—how much more happy she now is than we are, so that I might have wished to be traveling with her at this time. And this desire and this urge gave rise to a third solace, namely, that she is not lost forever, that we shall see her again and dwell together, more mirthfully and more happily than on this earth." And again in a letter to his father of April 4, 1787, on the occasion of the death of his friend, August von Hatzfeld, Mozart wrote: "He was just 31, like myself. I do not pity him but me, and from the depth of my heart. . . ."

Mozart was ailing throughout most of his life. His pale complexion, underlined by his blond hair, and his pointed nose signified that the body in which this powerful spirit had found an abode was doomed. Mozart had known about his illness for a long time. His condition, doubtless ascribable to overexertion, was fatal: "Excretory pyelitis with pyonephritis, latent focal lesions of the kidneys, tending inescapably toward eventual total nephritic insufficiency (Schenk)." Presentiments of death accompanied his creative endeavor, and when a mysterious messenger from Count von Walsegg arrived to commission a Requiem for an unknown person in the name of an unidentified patron, the master fell victim to the most profound pessimism and came to harbor the notion that power on high had ordered this song of death for him. A letter—presumably in answer to DaPonte's invitation to join him in London—shows Mozart aware of the imminent end and ready to accept it though he cannot feel that his life has run its full course. The phrase, "The hour strikes," is doubtless an allusion to the *Magic Flute* and seems influenced by masonic thought.

"My very dear Sir: I would fain follow your advice, but how shall I do so. My head is numb, I have trouble to make myself think, but the likeness of the Unknown leaves not my vision. I see him before me ever; he implores me, he urges me; he asks impatiently for the Work. I go on with it because composing is less tiring than idling. Elsewhere I have naught to fear. My condition tells me the hour strikes. I am about to expire my life. The end has come ere I could prove my talent. Yet life was beautiful. My career set out under prosperous signs. But we cannot change our destiny. We cannot count our days and must be resigned. The will of Providence be done. I close. The song of my death lies before me. I must not leave it unfinished.—Vienna, September 1791. Mozart."

Readers who are masons will be interested to learn about Mozart's intellectual culture. Niemetschek, the above-mentioned first biographer of Mozart, felt it regrettable that this rare artist was not also great in other phases of life. This observation reflects the high-brow philistinism of dawning Romanticism whose representatives, not unlike many of our contemporaries, found it difficult to understand that a great man need not be a paragon of every possible human virtue. In any event, we must and may think of Mozart as an educated man, a man of culture. In addition to German he felt at home in French, English, and Italian. He had read a great deal, and what he had read he had also taken in. It goes without saying, that his numerous tours had left no room for systematic attendance at a university. His educational level must not be compared with that of Bach or Handel or Telemann, Kuhnau, Philip Emanuel Bach. The Austrian musician had always been more of a music maker, while the North-German musician tended to be more of a musicologist. Indeed, in this matter Austria and Northern Germany are like color and line, like sensuousness and abstraction. Music flourishes in sensuousness; abstraction imposes limits upon it. Haydn too was hardly a person fit to satisfy the standards of individual culture of let us say Goethe and the romantics. All that Mozart had to offer was natural; nothing was the product of learning. He could have written his great works quite as well without the influence of contemporary and antecedent literature. As his training was not systematic but rather the product of fortuitous events, so we are not surprised to find that the library he left behind was a salmagundi of fiction, poetry, history, aesthetics, travel guides, juveniles, school texts, and almanacs. He had in his library the poetic works of Blumauer, Salomon Gessner, Ewald von Kleist, Christian Felix Weisse, and Wieland. Libretti and the dramatic genre were represented by Beaumarchais' *Figaro*, the Metastasio edition of 1781, and Molière's works. There were philosophical works of which we may mention Mendelssohn's *Phaedon*. The histories included the works of Frederick II and Mascow's *Introduction to the History of the Roman-German Empire*. Here we may also list the collected works of Sonnenfels. Mozart knew Gellert and Klopstock, but it is certain that he disliked the turgid output of the bards that was at least in part the result of the influence exerted by the poet of the Messias. This is evident from the fact that Mozart could not finish the musical setting he had begun of the turgid poem *Gibraltar* by Denis. It had nothing to offer that could have appealed to his sensitive ear. Did Mozart know the works of Lessing, Schiller, and Goethe? The texts of his German lieder are generally inferior concoctions, and he set but one poem of Goethe's to music. That is *The Violet*. But it is not even certain that he knew who had written the famous little poem from the ballad opera *Erwin and Elmire*, for it is possible that he found it in the collection brought out by the Austrian composer J. A. Steffan who ascribed it to Gleim. We cannot gainsay the regrettable inadequacy of Mozart's knowledge of literature. But this is a foible he shared with Haydn whose German lieder are similarly smitten with second- and third-rate texts. If it is true that Mozart was not widely read in poetry and fiction, he certainly was a passionate theater-goer. What else could we expect from the creator of *Idomeneo*, the *Abduction*, *Figaro, Don Giovanni*, and the *Magic Flute?* The numerous stock companies—Böhm's, Schikaneder's, etc.—that came to Salzburg, acquainted him with the works of the French classicists, the plays of Shakespeare, and Lessing's "Minna" and "Emilia Galotti." In Mannheim and later on in Vienna, Mozart conceived the idea that he might promote a national German Singspiel (or ballad opera), an endeavor which in a sense was ultimately fulfilled in the *Magic Flute*. In Paris he doubtless came in touch with the works of the Encyclopedists. Whether he actually read Voltaire, as has been inferred from his letter of July 3, 1778, is not certain. In any case, he regarded Voltaire as France's godless rationalism incar-

PLATE 7.
Masonic scene from the "Magic Flute" (1791) with Masonic
emblems (Vienna, Alberti 1791).

PLATE 8.

Scene of the Armored Men from the "Magic Flute" (Colored engraving by Joseph and Peter Schaffer, Vienna about 1793).

nate, and a passage like the following, from a letter of Mozart's to his father, is not easily reconciled with our knowledge that its writer came to be the creator of *Figaro*. "That the godless arch scoundrel Voltaire," he wrote, "dropped off like a dog, like a head of cattle—that is what he had coming." But we may assume that these biting remarks about Voltaire have to do with Mozart's bitter feelings toward Paris and above all with his falling out with his former friend, the Encyclopedist Melchior de Grimm. There are no allusions to Rousseau's death, which occurred at about the same time, although we can be quite certain that Mozart knew Rousseau's works, for in his little opera, *Bastien und Bastienne,* he used Mme. Favart's *Les Amours de Bastien et Bastienne,* which was a parody of Rousseau's *Devin du Village.* Mozart knew Grimm's *Correspondence Littéraire* and the little opera brochure by this same former patron of his, *Le Petit Prophète de Boehmisch-Broda.* Mozart did not own a regular musical library. His nomadic existence and countless changes of residence may explain why he never managed to accumulate a systematic collection of musical literature. Beethoven's case was not much different. In Mozart's records of personal effects there are listed but few works of music. Of the composers represented I may mention Michael Haydn, Gluck, Gassmann, Albrechtsberger, and Hofmeister. Mozart had not much use for theoretical works. His innermost personal inspiration was so abundant and rich a source that he could dispense with instruction from without, especially in his later years. From time to time he was obliged to listen to an opera by some other composer. As a rule, he was thoroughly bored on such occasions.

Some observations on Mozart's attitude toward nature may not be out of place. This covers his interest in landscapes and foreign lands, in which respect he is anything rather than a romanticist. We must remember that our modern feeling for nature has its roots in romantic conceptions. The powerful beauty of the Alps or the ocean is a thing which the average citizen of the eighteenth century could not grasp. In Haller's *The Alps* and in Goethe's *Italian Journey* we do find colorful descriptions of Alpine settings. But we must remember that both the elder and the younger Mozart could not but think of the Alps as a perfectly normal everyday phenomenon. A person who has spent his life within sight of the Untersberg and the Bavarian and Austrian Alpine ranges, may be excused for not being particularly impressed by a trip

119

through the central Alps, especially if we bear in mind what physical hardships such ventures involved in Mozart's time. Mozart, unlike Goethe, was not a man of three-dimensional sensuousness. He lived in the realm of sound. Time and again he complains about the discomforts of crossing the Alps. There is a lot of snow and a great deal of dirt. Bolzano is a "dirty hole," and the wild scenery can at best inspire him with a feeling of horror. The Italian landscape appeals to him through its graceful and gardenlike lines. He notes the fertility of the Italian soil and sees greater significance in this fact than in any temple of Jupiter. He passes by Mt. Vesuvius without any unusual display of interest, but he is fascinated by curios and relics of history. The Italian Baedeker of the eighteenth century (which Leopold had along like any other traveler) was Keyssler's description of his journeys with its pedestrian enumeration of historical sights and statistical deadweight. Mozart's feeling for nature is reflected in his music. Musical descriptions are comparatively rare, as for instance in *Idomeneo*. His representations of nature are more concerned with idyllic and graceful scenes, less with sublime and majestic effects, as is the case in Beethoven.

A Freemason like Mozart had to have a deep-rooted sense of friendship. He was sociable by nature and came to be a passionate bowler and billiard player. He also was an excellent dancer and loved trips to Vienna's Prater and the countryside nearby. He was always ready to participate in dancing parties and often helped out as choreographer and let himself be put in charge of other arrangements. "He danced the minuet with passionate devotion; at the ridottos he often wore character masks and excelled as Harlequin and Pierrot." (Nissen) A typical item is his letter of January 22, 1783, addressed to his father: "Last week I gave a ball at my home; of course, the stags paid two florins a piece; we started at 6 in the evening and stopped at 7. How is that again? Just one hour? Oh no, at 7 in the morning." In the same letter he asks his father for a harlequin's costume, and on March 12 of the same year he reports to his father on the production of a pantomime to which he had contributed both the conception and the music while the doggerel of the text was the work of the actor Müller. The numerous dances, minuets, allemandes, contradanses, and slow waltzes which Mozart wrote for the Viennese carnival balls reflect clearly his interest in Terpsichore's art, in which, as one source tells us, he was a past master if ever there was one. At darts, bowling, and billiards he had no peer. Like Beethoven, Mozart too was interested in horseback riding, but we should rather picture him as a leisurely Sunday afternoon horseman and not as a reckless jockey. In his earthy naturalness Mozart was fond of good food and liked a glass of wine with his meals. When there is no money, coffee and bread will do. But when cash comes in, it often gets invested in opulent parties. Yet Mozart was never a man of excesses. A person endowed with such social qualities had to develop a strong sense of friendship, and this of course was essential for him as a Freemason. His attachment to Haydn has already been mentioned. His letters to Gottfried Jacquin—the son of the Austrian botanist Nikolaus Joseph von Jacquin (1727-1817)—show him as a true friend, witness his unselfish readiness to let Gottfried take over compositions of his, completely relinquishing his rights of authorship. His relation to Count Hatzfeld was previously mentioned. Quite important, too, are his "table jesters," i.e., people that exploited him in a shameful way and ate their fill at his expense. The hornist Ignaz Leutgeb is an example. He played the horn for a living but also ran a cheese shop. Mozart dedicated to him a series of concertos for the horn. This good Salzburger was a bit of a simpleton, and Mozart made sure that he got at least a good laugh out of his dealings with him. To pay for one of his horn concertos, Leutgeb had to get down on all fours and gather together (and put in order) all the parts of Mozart's symphonies and concerts that were lying about the room in glorious disorder. Another horn concerto (K. 417) bears the inscription, "Wolfgang Amadé Mozart has taken pity on Leutgeb, the ass, ox, and fool, Vienna, May 27, 1783." Another one of those table jesters was Süssmayer, the man who later on completed the Requiem. And the clarinettist Stadler. As a friend Mozart was always ready to help. He often went beyond the limits of his own resource to help others out of a tight spot. So he made loans to his friend Franz von Gilowsky and also to Stadler. Like his sense of friendship was his love of animals. His dog Pimperl has come to share his immortality. At times Mozart kept such order in his papers that he did not forget to jot down the smallest item of expenditure. On May 1, 1784, he bought 2 May flowers for 1 kreuzer and on May 27, 1784, a starling bird for 34 kreuzers. Thereupon he wrote a melody with the notation: "That was beautiful." It was apparently the tune which the bird sang. He used it as the rondo theme in his concerto in G-major (K. 453). Now we are left with the question whether the bird got it from Mozart or Mozart from the bird.

The Eternal Feminine played an important part in Mozart's life. There is hardly another composer who found such ardent tones to speak of love of woman. Can anyone suppose that a genius who created the characters of Donna Anna, Countess Almaviva, Susan, and Zerlina, did not himself empty the cup of love to the last drop it could yield? Can anyone suppose that the man who created Don Giovanni and Cherubino, who painted in luxuriant colors the feelings of Don Giovanni, the Eternal Wanderer of Love, and the covetousness of Monostatos, can anyone suppose that that great man in early and more mature years escaped the spell of the demon the Greeks called Eros? It would be wrong to represent Mozart as a sort of Casanova and to call him a Don Giovanni. But there is something about him of a Cherubino who fluttered in tender love from one flower to the next. It is this fleeting indulgence for which his wife Konstanze coined the term "servant girleries." But it is true, at a later time Mozart admitted that he would be married a hundred times over if he had had to marry every girl with whom he had "given dalliance too much the rein." One such "dalliance" involved his cousin, the famous Bäsle Maria Anna Thekla, the daughter of Leopold's brother Franz Aloys. Wolfgang's letters to her seem to allude to all sorts of little adventures. They certainly are no reading matter for blushing girls. The Bäsle was no vestal virgin, as the birth out of wedlock of her daughter Maria Viktoria suffices to prove. But that was in 1793. Much more serious than Mozart's affair with Maria Anna was his love for Aloysia Weber in Mannheim in 1777. This 16-year-old beauty, endowed with a magnificent voice and a wonderful sense of music, enchanted the young genius to such an extent that he could think of nothing but of the urgent need to tie her to himself forever. Yet Luise (as she was called) was a real flirt who granted poor Mozart only such favors as her mother thought suitable, and when Prince Elector Charles Theodore accorded her in 1778 at Munich a high leading lady's income, she cut Mozart dead. Later on she married the actor and painter Joseph Lange, though after a while she grew tired of him and ran away. As everybody knows, Mozart married in the end Aloysia's sister Konstanze. She was in his life a good friend and a good companion, though perhaps in matters of conjugal fidelity she was not always a model of meticulousness. In any case, Mozart was happy with her. It is certain that her utter lack of talent in matters economic caused the master many a bitter day and forced him to push his musical productivity to the breaking point. She did contribute to the master's all too early demise. Konstanze never made him forget his truly great love, Aloysia. As late as May 16, 1781, he wrote about her: "I loved her . . . and I feel that she still means something to me. It is lucky that her husband is a jealous fool and does not allow her to go anywhere so that I get to see her only rarely." As sentimental as Mozart was in regard to Luise, so realistic were his sensations in regard to his cousin Anna Maria. In one of his letters to her he paraphrases a sentimental ode by Klopstock in these terms:

> Thy sweet likeness, o cousin,
> Hovers before my mind's eye.
> I see thee when the lights
> Of day fall. When the moon
> Shines for me, I see thee—and weep
> For it is not thy self . . .

> Finis coronat opus!
> S.V.P.T.
> Knight of Boarstail.

During Mozart's life and shortly after his death much was said about his libertinism. Certain escapades and servant girleries may have happened. But nothing has been demonstrated for certain. Even in the matter of the ill-famed scandal about Frau Hofdemel —Kapellmeister Pokorny's daughter Magdalene—Mozart's innocence has been completely vindicated. Franz Hofdemel, the former secretary of a certain Count Seilern, was to be initiated into the lodge "Newly Crowned Hope" ("Zur neugekrönten Hoffnung"). At this time Mozart had approached him once again for a loan, as we know from the letter of April, 1789, in which Mozart alluded to the forthcoming initiation. Five days after Mozart's death, Hofdemel tried to kill his wife and then committed suicide. The case was linked to an affair which Mozart was supposed to have had with Frau Hofdemel. Mozart's innocence was established, but rumors continued to proliferate. Much later Beethoven refused to play in the presence of Frau Hofdemel because "she had that mixup with Mozart." Much more serious were Mozart's feelings for Anna Selina Storace (Nancy). And if we may lend credence to the sounds of the soprano aria, "Ch'io mi scordi di te" (K. 505)—Mozart wrote in the thematic catalogue, "For Demoiselle Storace and myself"—then his feelings for her must have amounted to glowing veneration. "It is a duet of voice and piano with accompaniment, an avowal of love in sounds, the sublimation of a relationship that could not be consummated." (Einstein)

Political views are often taken as an essential criterion in the judgment passed on a Freemason. That Mozart referred to himself occasionally as an arch-Englishman has been mentioned before. He actually fell victim to a sort of anglomania, and as late as 1787—when he quietly considered the possibility of making Britain his permanent home—he took up the study of the English language. Kronauer's masonic guest book with an English quotation in Mozart's own hand tells us much about his anglophile attitude. His views on France were much less friendly, for his appreciation of French music was rather cool. In the correspondence of father and son we find numerous political comments, and some of these make us smile through their naive ingenuousness. It seems that Leopold was an anti-militarist, as may be judged by a letter of his written from Württemberg on July 11, 1763: "You can hardly spit without spitting into an officer's pocket or a soldier's cartridge pouch. You hear all the time in the streets: 'Halt! March! Wheel!' And nothing is to be seen but arms, drums, equipment." And Wolfgang wrote on December 18, 1778 from Kaisersheim: "The most ridiculous thing, to my mind, is all that military humbug. I wish I knew what it is good for. At night I always hear, 'Who is there?' And I always answer, 'So what?' " On the whole it seems that the Mozarts were interested in small political gossip and much less in great historical happenings. Discussions like those which Beethoven had with Grillparzer on the question of political freedom in the United States were hardly to be met with in Mozart's circle.

We also must clear Mozart of the suspicion of antisemitism. This point has its antecedents in a letter which Wolfgang wrote on September 11, 1782, to Leopold. In it he mentions the sensational espionage case of Eleonore Eskeles. She was the daughter of

124

a rabbi and was unjustly accused of having obtained political secrets from the officer Johann Valentin Günther, a freemason, ministerial secretary, and representative of the Emperor, and of having turned these secrets over to Prussian spies. In his letter Mozart called the girl a "capital sow," but this is a remark we need not take too seriously. In truth, Mozart had excellent relations with the Jewish Baron Raimund Wetzlar, the builder of the Seitenstatt Temple in Vienna. Wetzlar was partly responsible for Mozart's connection with DaPonte. In London the Mozarts were fairly close to the Jewish cellist Sipontini whom Leopold actually tried to convert to Catholicism. That there was no racial antisemitism at the time is obvious. Otherwise Mozart could never have worked with DaPonte whose real name was Emanuele Conegliano (Corduan Gerber) while his mother was Chela Pincherle and hailed from the ghetto of Ceneda. If Mozart's times had known the sickness of racial antisemitism, we would not have *Don Giovanni, Figaro,* and *Cosi fan tutte* and would be the poorer for it.

Much has been made of Mozart's nationalism and patriotism. It is true, he had the ideal of creating a German opera, and the well-known letter to Anton von Klein in Mannheim (which Frau Ludendorff interpreted so creatively as proof of Mozart's having been poisoned by the freemasons) was concerned with the establishment and maintenance of a German opera in Vienna. It is possible that Mozart felt instinctively that the pinnacle of his dramatic endeavor could only be reached in a German opera. That it turned out to be simultaneously a German and a masonic opera is one of the most remarkable phenomena of history.

MASONIC MUSIC AFTER MOZART

THE MUSIC of the classical period has been called the art of liberalism and idealism. Mozart expressed the same ideals of universal brotherhood, humanism, and deism in his great symphonies, in the *Magic Flute,* and, above all, in his Masonic compositions. In Beethoven's middle period these principles reached their high-water mark. For while Mozart had to accommodate the Salzburg archbishop and knew real freedom only during the last few years of his life, Beethoven felt himself a free artist throughout his career. In contrast to Mozart, Beethoven was a revolutionary who wanted to change the ways of the world and, like Goethe and Schiller in their period of "storm and stress," presented a front of defiance to the gods and his fate. Although he lost his hearing as a young man, Beethoven not only continued with his art but climbed the highest peaks of musical creation. "It is strength which sets man above all other creatures," or "one must grasp fate by the horns." Not only did he live in accordance with these sayings, he also composed by them. For they bring to a victorious conclusion the battle with human fate as well as with the demon in one's own breast. This optimism can be felt in the last movements of his great symphonies, the *Eroica,* the fifth and the ninth. The victory of humanity and universal brotherhood are his *Leitmotifs.* Works like *Egmont, Fidelio,* and the ninth symphony are the musical expression of German idealism as preached by Kant and Fichte.

For Beethoven, the creator of the universe was not the biblical God, but a great and incomprehensible being which he called, characteristically, "the deity" *(Gottheit),* even in letters to the Cardinal Archbishop, Archduke Rudolf, for whose enthronement he composed the *Missa Solemnis.* "There is nothing greater in life," he wrote to this pupil and patron in 1823, "than to get nearer the deity than other mortals, and to diffuse its light among men." In 1820, he wrote in his notebook, in large letters: "The

126

moral law within us and the starry heaven above us—Kant! ! !"
Kant's Categorical Imperative was his motto throughout his life.
He was the incarnation of Masonic ethics and philosophy, a
"Mason without badge." Characteristically, his setting of Schiller's
Ode to Joy, perhaps his greatest work, had been planned for many
years and was finally used at the end of the ninth symphony. Like
a titan with clenched fists, he massed and formed the sounds of
jubilation for all mankind to share.

We have no way of knowing whether Beethoven was a Mason.
Thayer, Deiters, and Riemann took it for granted and assumed
that he discontinued his lodge visits only when he lost his hearing.
Hérriot, former French Premier and mayor of Lyons, is also certain of it. In his book about the composer, he calls attention to a
letter written by Beethoven concerning the death of his brother
Karl, a letter which mentions the acacia, a Masonic symbol (at
Masonic funerals acacia branches are thrown into the grave). In
a letter to Wegeler, written May 2, 1810, Beethoven mentions a
Masonic song, asking his friend to send it to him. He vaguely
remembered having composed such a song in Bonn. Wegeler, in
his *Biographische Notizen,* says that Beethoven was mistaken, that
it was a sacrificial song by Matthisson on which a Masonic text had
been superimposed. Wegeler himself did this with Beethoven's
song, *Wer ist ein freier Mann,* and both of these texts are printed
in the appendix of *Biographische Notizen* and are still occasionally
sung at lodge meetings. It is equally uncertain whether Schindler,
Beethoven's friend and biographer, was a member of the Craft.
Beethoven sometimes referred to him as a "Samothracian," that is,
a member of the Samothracian Order. At Schindler's first visit
to Beethoven they exchanged a hand-shake which may have been
a Masonic sign, and Schindler wrote, "a handshake explained the
rest." It is possible that Beethoven in his youth had belonged to
a lodge in the Rhineland. But in Vienna, where the lodges had
ceased to function after the death of Joseph II, he would have had
no opportunity to attend meetings and presumably he forgot his
Masonic past. He may have been introduced into the lodge by his
teacher, Neefe.

There were many Masons among later German musicians: Abt,
Damrosch, Lindpaintner, Litolff, Löwe, Lortzing, Reissiger,
Speyer, and Spohr. Löwe was a member of the lodge "Zu den
drei Zirkeln" (three compasses) in Stettin, into which he was

initiated in 1829, and for which he composed several Masonic quartets. His most popular song, *Die Uhr* (the clock) was first performed at a lodge meeting. Lortzing joined the lodge "Zur Beständigkeit und Eintracht" (constancy and harmony) in Aachen in 1826, and, in 1834, became affiliated with the lodge "Balduin zur Linde." For the 100th anniversary of the lodge "Minerva zu den drei Palmen" in Leipzig, in 1841, he composed a jubilee cantata.

In more recent years, German musicians who belonged to the Craft included Gerhard von Keussler, Alexander Zemlinsky, and Theodor Veidl. Keussler and Veidl made musical contributions to Masonry. Hugo Riemann was a member of the lodge "Phönix" in Leipzig, where, as Entered Apprentice or Master, he gave a lecture, *Warum ist die Musik eine so hochgeschätzte Gehilfin der königlichen Kunst?* (why is music so valuable an aid to Masonry?) See *Latomia*, 1897, p. 209.

Richard Wagner's connection with the Craft is of considerable interest. Apparently he had been introduced to Masonry by Liszt, who had been initiated into the lodge "Zur Einigkeit" (unity) in Frankfurt in 1841 under the sponsorship of Speyer. Liszt had attained the second and third degrees in the lodge "Zur Eintracht" in Berlin. But Wagner's interest was aroused even more by his brother-in-law, the husband of his sister Rosalie, Dr. Oswald Marbach, member of the Leipzig lodge "Balduin zur Linde" and editor of a Masonic periodical, *Am Reissbrett* (at the drawing-board). In Bayreuth, the banker Friedrich Feustel, a member of the lodge "Aloysius zur Verschwiegenheit" (Aloysius, to silence) and master of the Grand lodge "Zur Sonne" (sun) in Bayreuth, played a decisive part in the creation of the Festival Theater and also encouraged Wagner's interest in Freemasonry.

Documents of the Bayreuth lodge indicate that Wagner intended to join, but was prevented by considerations of private matters, such as his relationship to Hans von Bülow and a disinclination to offend Bavarian Catholic circles. Nevertheless, some Masonic terms and ideas appear in *Parsifal,* for example, the expression "high noon" and the responsorial organization of the Grail scene.

Among the Masonic musicians in Italy we find Sarti, Scalabrini, Mingotti, Puccini, Boito; in Norway, Ole Bull; in Poland, Elsner; in Czechoslovakia, Kociàn and Nedbal; in the United States, Cadman, Sousa, Whiteman, Irving Berlin, and Marshal Kernochan; and the list could continue. Jean Sibelius is also a Freemason, having joined the Grand Lodge of Finland in Helsinki in 1923, a lodge which, until 1933, operated under the patronage of the Grand Lodge of New York. When the Finnish lodge gained its independence it presented the New York lodge with the manuscript score of Sibelius's *Masonic Music,* with words in Swedish and Finnish. In an English translation by Marshal Kernochan, this work was published by the Grand Lodge of New York. It contains three pieces for male quartet, pieces for tenor with piano accompaniment, and a funeral march for meetings of the third degree. One of these was performed by a New York choir of 500 voices under Hugh Ross in New York on May 1, 1938, with a secular text entitled "Onward, ye Peoples." The work was a great success and is now in the repertory of most American choirs. It is composed in Sibelius's personal style, but it also contains some elements of Mozart's humanitarian style.

Research into the history of Freemasonry continues in the lodges of Europe, carried out by professional and amateur scholars. In England it is cultivated by the *Quatuor Coronati* lodge, and in the United States by the American Lodge of Research.

FOOTNOTES

MOZART AND THE CRAFT

[1]Koch, B. *Mozart, Freimaurer und Illuminaten.*

[2]*Quellenlexikon.*

[3]This is disputed by O. E. Deutsch.

[4]*Geschichte der Freimaurerei in Österreich-Ungarn.*

[5]This whole matter can be easily explained by the irreverent rationalism of the period.

[6]Karl Friedrich Hensler, masonic writer, whose play, *Handeln macht den Mann oder Die Freimaurer* (deeds make the man, or the Freemasons) appeared in 1784, and whose Singspiel, *Das Sonnenfest der Brahminen* (the sun festival of the Brahmins) was set to music by Wenzel Müller.

[7]The complete funeral oration, with allusions to the third degree, was first reprinted by O. E. Deutsch in *Schweizerische Musikzeitung*, Feb., 1956, and again in Nettl, *Mozart als Freimaurer und Mensch* (Hamburg, 1956).

[8]Note the similarity to the close of Sarastro's "Aria of Revenge."

MASONIC MUSIC BEFORE MOZART

[1]Johann Christopher Pepusch (1667-1752), born in Berlin, composer of the famous *Beggar's Opera* which cleaned up the *opera seria* of Handel and Bononcini in England.

[2]For a more complete list of English and American Masonic song books, see L. B. Blakemore, *Masonic Lodge Methods* (Chicago, 1953). The chapter on music in this book does not mention the name of Mozart.

MASONIC MUSICIANS AROUND MOZART

[1]The portion of the speech directed specifically to Haydn: "It is superfluous to describe to you, our new Brother Apprentice, the charms of that heavenly being, harmony. You already know so well her great power in one of the most beautiful branches of human knowledge. This lovable goddess seems to have given you part of her sweet, magical

powers with which to calm the turbulent soul, to lull to sleep pain and sorrow, to shorten the melancholy hours and lift up the spirit to great and noble heights. I shall be content if I have succeeded, through my brotherly advice, in persuading you to remain faithful to your dear friend, even in this new domain. I shall be even happier and shall feel that I have achieved my purpose if I have convinced my Brothers how indispensable is this fundamental virtue of Masons. May they continue to attentively follow every sign given them by this gracious goddess."

THE MAGIC FLUTE: BACKGROUND

¹Story of the opera: Act I.

Pursued by a monstrous serpent, Tamino hurries down from the rocks and faints. His cries for help were heard by three ladies dressed in black, who enter and kill the serpent with their spears. They reluctantly leave the beautiful youth. When Tamino regains consciousness, he sees dancing toward him an extraordinary figure, dressed completely in feathers and carrying an enormous bird cage. It is Papageno, the bird-catcher, who informs Tamino that he is now in the realm of the Queen of the Night. He also tells Tamino that it was he, Papageno, who killed the monster. He is immediately punished for this lie by the three ladies, who reappear and fasten a padlock to his mouth. To Tamino they give a small picture of a girl with whose beauty he immediately falls in love. Now the Queen of the Night herself appears to him and tells him that the picture represents her daughter, Pamina, who has been abducted by the wicked sorcerer Sarastro. Tamino has been chosen to rescue her, and her hand shall be his reward. The Queen disappears and the three ladies return, remove the padlock from Papageno's mouth, and present him with a magic glockenspiel. To Tamino they give a magic flute which is to help him overcome the dangers of their journey, on which they will be accompanied by the three genii.

In the second scene we see a richly furnished room in Sarastro's palace. The ugly Negro, Monostatos, is trying to make love to Pamina, but Papageno's appearance frightens him away. The bird-catcher recognizes Pamina and tells her that her rescue is near. In the third scene, the three genii have conducted Tamino into a grove in which there are three temples. When he approaches the first two, a loud voice commands him to stand back. A priest steps from the third temple and tells him that Sarastro is not a wicked sorcerer but noble and full of wisdom. Tamino, he says, will understand the truth only when "friendship leads him by the hand to join the Temple's sacred band." Tamino is pondering all this, strangely moved, when he hears Papageno's glockenspiel. In answer to Tamino's flute, Papageno and Pamina appear but begin to run away. They are intercepted by Monostatos and several slaves, but Papageno's glockenspiel charms them and compels them to dance. Sarastro's approach is now heralded by trumpets. Pamina sinks down at his feet and tells him that the Negro's love-making has driven her to flight. Just then Monostatos drags in Tamino, but, instead of being rewarded, the Negro is sentenced to a beating. Tamino and Pamina are taken to one of the temples; they are to show whether they are worthy of the great happiness in store for them.

Act II.

In a palm grove Sarastro tells the priests his plans. The gods have destined Tamino and Pamina for each other. But as Tamino was yet to be tested, Sarastro had removed Pamina from her mother, the Queen of the Night, the patroness of darkness and superstition. Tamino and Pamina have to withstand several difficult tests before they are worthy of entering the Temple of Light. These fabulous tests, which Tamino passes by his own virtue, with the aid of the magic flute, and finally with the help of Pamina, follow. Papageno fails and does not gain admission, but is given Papagena for a wife. Darkness has been conquered. The young couple enter the Temple of the Sun.

[2] Richard Engländer, *Joh. Gottlieb Naumann.* Leipzig 1922.

[3] See also Viktor Junk, *Goethes Fortsetzung der Zauberflöte.*

[4] *Sethos,* I, page 37.

[5] The dress is very reminiscent of the Masonic costume, especially the chain around the neck, the so-called "Bijou," which ordinarily contains a Masonic emblem, the figure of truth.

[6] The actual initiates.

[7] *Wolfgang Amadeus Mozart,* II, p. 765.

[8] Reprinted in *Mozarteums-Mitteilungen,* 1919.

[9] Cf. the above-mentioned letter of Seyfried.

[10] On October 7, 1791, Mozart wrote to his wife: "What pleases me most is their quiet approval." Alfred Meissner asserts that his grandfather, G. A. Meissner, member of the lodge "Zur Wahrheit und Einigkeit" in Prague, had met the composer on his last visit there, and had reported that Mozart on that occasion had promised his brothers a great Masonic composition.

THE MAGIC FLUTE: WORDS AND MUSIC

[1] According to Winterstein, *Ursprung der Tragödie,* early Greek tragedy was probably simply a cult of rebirth, and this may also be true of the Egyptian initiation rites.

THE MAGIC FLUTE: SEQUELS

[1] See also the role of the coffin in the Osiris myth.

NOTES

See Lenning, *Allgem. Handbuch der Freimaurerei* (Leipzig, 1901); Eugen Lennhoff and Oskar Posner, *Internationales Freimaurer Lexikon* (Vienna, 1932). (p. 5)

Gregor Schwartz-Bostunitsch, *Die Freimaurerei* (Weimar: Alexander Duncker Verlag, 1928). About the relationships of Ludendorff and his wife to Freemasonry, see the appropriate article in Lennhoff and Posner. (p. 6)

Franz Xaver von Bader (or Baader), 1785-1841, theosophist and Master of the Illuminati lodge in Munich. (p. 9ff)

Adam Weisshaupt, born 1748 in Ingolstadt, died 1830. Adolf, Freiherr von Knigge, 1752-1796, the famous author of *Ueber den Umgang mit Menschen*, adopted strict observance and corresponded with its leaders and the Rosicrucians. See Ferd. Josef Schneider, *Die Freimaurerei und ihr Einfluss auf die geistige Kultur in Deutschland am Ende des 18. Jahrhunderts* (Prague, 1909).

Carl Theodor, Elector of the Palatinate and Bavaria, 1724-1799, at whose courts in Mannheim and Munich Mozart was repeatedly active without, however, attaining the position for which he strove.

Friedrich Franz Joseph Spaur, 1756-1841, canon at Salzburg, a position which he also held at Brixen and Passau, and finally *Domdechant* at Salzburg. See the references given by Wurzbach, *Biographisches Lexikon des Kaiserthums Oesterreich*. He was the oldest son of the Imperial judge Franz Joseph at Innsbruck as well as nephew of the Bishop of Brixen, Joseph Philipp, and the former Bishop, Ignaz Joseph (1729-1779), with whom the Mozarts had some contact. Beginning in 1763 he was co-adjutor of his uncle Leopold Joseph (1696-1778) in Brixen. For Ignaz, Mozart composed one of his most beautiful masses, the so-called Credo Mass or Spaur Mass (see Schenk, *W. A. Mozart*, p. 267). (p. 10ff)

Wolfegg, Count Anton Willibald (1729-1820), president of the *Hofkammer* and humanist, from 1762 on canon at Salzburg, but not ordained until 1778. One of the greatest philanthropists of his time, he died in poverty of his own free will. In 1777 he was among the admirers of Mozart's *Klavier* playing at Augsburg, having already heard the master in 1768 at the home of Prince Galitzin in Vienna. In 1778 he participated as a cellist in the amateur orchestra founded in Salzburg by Count Czernin (see Wurzbach). (p. 11)

Schelle, Augustin, learned Benedictine (1742-1805), professor of ethics, natural law, history, and oriental languages at the university, later director of the university library and rector of the university (see Wurzbach).

Johann Nepomuk, Count Spaur (1724-1793), prefect and *Burggraf* of Tyrol (see Wurzbach).

Gilowsky, Joseph Anton Ernst (1739-1787), the older cousin of Maria Anna Katharina Gilowsky (1750-1802), who appears frequently in Mozart's correspondence. She was the daughter of the *Antecamera-Kammerdiener* Wenzel Andreas Gilowsky of Urazowa (1716-1799). Franz Wenzel (1757-1816) was the brother of "Katherl." (p. 11)

Hübner, Lorenz (1753-1807), a former Jesuit, from 1784 on editor of the *Oberteutsche Staatszeitung*, in connection with which appeared the *Salzburger Intelligenzblatt*, monthly scholarly contributions to the literature of Upper Austria. The *Staatszeitung* was suppressed by Elector Carl Theodor because of its liberal tone. Hübner, an exponent of Salzburg rationalism, appears repeatedly in the correspondence between Leopold Mozart and his daughter (see Wurzbach).

Concerning Amann: Deutsch *(Leop. Mozarts Briefe an seine Tochter)* also mentions the Salzburg captain Dominicus von Amann (died March 3, 1791), whose father presumably was the councillor of the exchequer Franz Anton von Amann.

The letter of Leopold to his daughter was first published in my book *Mozart und die königliche Kunst* (1932) and again by Otto Erich Deutsch and Bernhard Paumgartner in *Leopold Mozarts Briefe an seine Tochter.* (p. 12)

Clam-Gallas, Count Christian Phillip, died 1805, patron of the Prague singer Josepha Duschek, for whom Wolfgang composed the Soprano Arias K. 272 and K. 528, in whose Villa Bertramka *Don Giovanni* was completed, and for whom Beethoven wrote the concert aria *A Perfido.*

Dr. Johann Hutterer (or Hutter), University notary and *Hofratsadvokat*. His arrest occurred during a conflict between the Archbishop and the Salzburg peasantry, whom Hutterer was representing. Note the reserve with which Leopold Mozart refers to Masonry.

For the following, cf. Ludwig Abafi, *Geschichte der Freimaurerei in Oesterreich-Ungarn* (Budapest, 1893). (p. 12)

The author of *Josephinische Curiosa* is Franz Gräffer (1785-1852). See Gräffer, *Kleine Wiener Memoiren und Wiener Dosenstücke*, edited by Schlossar and Gugitz (Munich, 1918). (p. 13)

The quotation of Pezzl is taken from Dr. Adolf Deutsch, *Sammlung von Wiener Schattenrissen aus dem Jahre 1784* (Vienna, 1928).

For the history of the Viennese lodges in their relationship to Mozart, see Otto Erich Deutsch, *Mozart und die Wiener Logen* (Vienna, 1932).

Ignaz von Born, geologist and mineralogist (1742-1791). He was born in Karlsburg, Transylvania, became an advisor to the *Münz-und Bergmeisteramt* in Prague in 1770, and made scientific expeditions within the country. From 1779 on he was *Hofrat* of the *Hofkammer* in coinage and mining matters.

See Johann Pezzl, *Lebensbeschreibung Montecucculis, W. Lichtensteins und Borns* (Vienna, 1792) and the references given by Wurzbach. About Born, see also Edwin Zellweker, *Das Urbild des Sarastro* (Vienna, 1953). Among the intellectual members mentioned, Michael Denis, custodian of the court library (1729-1800) was the poet of "Calpe" (Gibraltar), which Mozart intended to set to music, a plan which was not carried through because of the bombastic and Ossianic character of the poem. After 1783, Born edited a scholarly masonic journal, *Physikalische Arbeiten der einträchtigen Freunde in Wien*. Each of the scientists contributed writings in his specialty; for example, Born wrote on mineralogy, zoology, and related fields, Denis on botany and entomology, Pacassi on mathematics, etc. See articles on these scholars by Wurzbach. Another periodical, incited by a member of "Zur wahren Eintracht," Joseph von Sonnenfels, a man of Jewish descent who was one of the main representatives of Austrian enlightenment, and edited by the poet Aloys Blumauer, was the *Journal für Freymäurer*, published 1784-1786 as a manuscript without censorship in twelve volumes quarto. The contribution of greatest interest to us is Born's essay on the mysteries of the ancient Egyptians. Other prominent members of the "Eintracht" lodge were Joseph Barth, anatomist and physician of Joseph II; Johann Nepomuk Hunczowsky, staff surgeon, teacher of surgery, later Imperial surgeon, and for a time the physician of Mozart and Beethoven (see Nettl, "Zu einem Puchberg-Brief," *Acta Mozartiana* II, 1955); Joseph Märter, scientist, who spent the years 1784 and 1785 in America; the physicist Franz Jäger; *Generalmajor* and *Feldmarschall-Leutnant* Cornelius von Ayrenhoff, a dramatist and writer who edited an anonymous piece, *Ueber die theatralischen Tänze* in 1794; Anton and Bartolomäus von Tinti whom we also know from Mozart's biography; Johann Ferdinand Deurer, Protestant preacher; the famous physician and professor Johann Peter Frank; Councillor Franz von Greiner, father of Caroline Pichler; the writer Johann Friedrich Schink. By no means does this exhaust the large list of the Viennese intellectual leaders who assembled in Born's lodge. Nevertheless we cannot deny that a part of the scientific discussions held under Born's leadership were devoted to alchemy, especially to the artificial manufacture of gold. The fact that Born withdrew from the Craft in August of 1786 does not exclude the possibility that he was Schikaneder's model for Sarastro.

About the *Josephinische Freimaurerpatent* and the "masonic revolution" connected with it, see Abafi, vol. III, p. 143. (p. 14)

Gemmingen, Otto, Baron of Hornberg and Treschklingen, born in Heilbronn, came to Mannheim as Electoral treasurer, edited *Mannheimische Dramaturgie* for the year 1779. Mozart had the Quartet K. 80, the Quintet K. 174, and the Fischer-Variations K. 179 copied for him and received 3 *louis d'ors* and a recommendation for them (see Schenk, *W. A. Mozart*, p. 412). Gemmingen joined the lodge "Zur gekrönten Hoffnung" in 1782, but left it, along with seven other brothers, on Jan. 15, 1783, and founded the lodge "Zur Wohltätigkeit" on Feb. 2. He is represented in the Kronauer album.

Leopold Aloys Hoffmann (1748-1806), son of a German-Bohemian tailor, and at first sponsored by Michael Denis. Gemmingen introduced him into the circle of Freemasons and Illuminati. He enjoyed the favor of van Swieten who obtained for him a professorship of German language at the University of Pest. There Hoffmann stayed until 1790, when he returned to Vienna to become professor and *Rat* at the university. In 1786 he published a brochure entitled *Kaiser Josephs Reformation der Freimaurer,* referring to an expression used by the Emperor and mocking some of the customs of his former brothers. After the death of Joseph he changed sides and became a professional spy and informer. The belief that Freemasonry was identical with Jacobinism is largely due to the publications of Hoffmann. His criminal activities ended in 1792, with the death of Emperor Leopold. Hoffmann himself died, scorned by the world, in Wiener Neustadt (see Wurzbach and Nagl-Zeidler, *Deutsch-oesterreichische Literaturgeschichte* [Vienna, 1914]). (p. 15)

Announcement of the lodge "Zur Wohltätigkeit" to the sister-lodges in Vienna:

Proposed: Conductor Mozart—Our former Secretary Brother Hoffmann forgot to notify the worthy sister lodges of this proposal, the Petitioner has been announced at the honorable district lodge for four weeks, and we wish to proceed with his initiation next week if the worthy sister lodges have no objection.

57 5 84   Schwanckhardt: Secretary
XII

In another entry into the minutes of the lodge "Eintracht" on April 22, 1785, the names of Leopold and Wolfgang Mozart appear as visiting brothers; Leopold's name is crossed out, presumably because he, as a Fellow Craft, could not attend a meeting of third degree masons. We can assume that the intimacy between Haydn and Mozart is due to their common masonic experience. Cf. the Italian dedication to Haydn in the third edition of the Köchel catalogue, p. 506. (cf. p. 111)

We should point out that the lack of correspondence between father and son from the time after 1785 may have reasons unrelated to masonry. Perhaps Konstanze destroyed some letters of Leopold's, critical of Wolfgang's marriage, together with the replies. (p. 18)

Anton David and Vincent Springer were outstanding clarinettists who specialized on the basset-horn, an alto clarinet in F. Theodor Lotz, violist and first clarinettist with Batthyany in Bratislava, improved the basset-horn. He may have been the contrabassoonist in the invitation. Springer played a *Concertante* for two basset-horns with Dworzack at a benefit for Haydn, in London on May 16, 1791, and his colleague David played another duet for these instruments with Signor Pachierotti.

Joseph Paul Weinbrenner (1728-1807), Vienna industrialist and fur dealer, was also prominent in textiles and printing. He was responsible for the opening of the first normal school in Austria, in 1771. His home was a gathering-place of the most important scholars and artists of Vienna.

Besides Born, the names of other famous Masons are included: Sonnenfels, Greiner, Ployer, Puthon, Weinbrenner, Engeström (Acad. Subscribers). (p. 19)

A further masonic associate of Mozart's was the *Justizkanzlist* Franz Hofdemel in Vienna, who loaned the composer 100 Gulden. A letter written in the beginning of April, 1789, includes the following passage: "Soon we shall be able to call each other by a more beautiful name! Your affair is near its conclusion." This indicates that Hofdemel was a Petitioner, presumably of the lodge "Zur Neugekrönten Hoffnung." Nevertheless, Hofdemel had Mozart issue a promissory note. Hofdemel is the subject of a story published in the sensational newspaper *Heimlicher Botschafter*. Shortly after Mozart's death a family tragedy took place in Hofdemel's house. Hofdemel wounded his pregnant wife and then killed himself. The reason given was that Mozart, who had again borrowed money from Hofdemel, had been on intimate terms with the latter's wife. Indeed, the child was named Johann Wolfgang Amadeus Franz, the first names of both Mozart and Hofdemel. Beethoven was aware of this affair. (cf. p. 123) (p. 20)

Canal, Joseph Emanuel, Count of Malabaila (1745-1826), officer and humanist. He was partially responsible for the founding of the St. John's orphanage in Prague, and built one of the most famous botanical gardens of Europe. He had his private musical organization (See Wurzbach, and Nettl, *Mozart in Böhmen*).

Ungar, Karl Raphael (1743-1807), born in Saaz, originally Karl Unger. In 1780, he became director of the university library, in 1788 a secular priest, and later imperial councillor. He was one of the most important promoters of the university library in Prague. The negotiations concerning the founding of the lodge "Zur Wahrheit und Einigkeit," which were undertaken by Born, took place in 1783. He could not have encountered Mozart through Masonry at that time (see Schenk, p. 668).

The poem was reprinted for the first time by Gustav Brabbée in the *Wiener Freimaurerzeitung*. (p. 23)

This is the last known letter written by Mozart to his father. However, since Leopold, in a letter of May 10 to Nannerl gives a new address of Wolfgang's, Landstrasse 244, and since Leopold frequently wrote to his daughter, we can assume that several letters have disappeared. Leopold died on May 28, 1787, at the age of 68, of consumption, and was buried at the St. Sebastian cemetery in Salzburg. (p. 23)

The album was also published in facsimile by the firm Jaffé in Vienna (now New York). Since only a few copies were printed the facsimile is also very rare. Among the members of the lodge "Zur gekrönten Hoffnung," the following are worth mentioning: August or Rudolf Gräffer, both book dealers and publishers, the latter associated with the poet Blumauer; Otto Baron Gemmingen; the painter Ignaz Unterberger, member of the Academy of Arts; Count Franz Esterhazy, for whom Mozart composed the *Masonic Funeral Music* (K. 477); Alexander, Baron of Proney (1760-1839), later general inspector of the Lutheran church in Hungary and a well-known writer; Pasquale Artaria, art dealer and music publisher (1755-1785); Wenzel Tobias Epstein; Tobias Philipp von Gebler, commander of the order of St. Stephen (1726-1786) for whose drama *König Thamos* (K. 345) Mozart composed the choruses; the musicians Joseph Bartha, Vittorio Colombazzo, and Ferdinand

Schleiss; Joseph Pasqualati (1733-1799), whose sons were acquainted with Beethoven; the actor and tenor Valentin Adamberger; the dancing-master Karl Prandstetter; the Bohemian secular priest and poet Franz Petran. (p. 24)

Among the Viennese court ballet masters, the most important was the choreographer Franz Hilverding van Wewen (1710-1786), member of the Vienna lodge "Zu den drei Kanonen." Frank Bernhart of London, who possesses a facsimile of the album, points out that Born's name does not appear in Kronauer's index, and that the letters "L.B." indicate that the name was added later. Bernhart also asserts that Alxinger's entry *Rara est concordia fratrum* is to be translated in its 18th century sense, namely, with the word *rara* meaning "noble." But in this connection we should mention the disagreements among the Viennese lodges of the time. Furthermore, Leopold Mozart had participated in a Jesuit play, *Rara fratrum concordia*, in Augsburg at the age of nine.

The pinnacle of Müller's career was the commission in 1776 to travel through Germany in order to secure competent personnel for the newly founded *Nationalbühne* (see the autobiography of Joseph Lange, Mozart's brother-in-law, published in Vienna in 1808, which described Müller's departure from the theater). The masonic associations of Müller to Mozart are proved in a letter of Leopold to his daughter, written from Vienna on Feb. 21, 1785. Since Leopold was being considered for initiation into the lodge "Wohltätigkeit" at that time, Müller's invitation of the Mozart family can easily be explained. The Mozarts took part in a meal for 21 persons. (p. 26)

Lorenz von Engström or Engeström, Swedish ambassador at the court. (p. 27)

Joseph Martin Kraus (1756-1792). His autobiography in Swedish appeared in Stockholm, in 1833. In 1778 he worked at the Stockholm theater, and from 1781 he was conductor there. In 1782 he embarked on a journey of several years to Vienna, Italy, Paris, and London, and returned to Stockholm on Jan. 1, 1787. In 1788 he was Swedish court conductor (see Eitner, *Quellenlexikon*).

Joseph Zistler, "a truly soulful violinist, whose rich tone and intensive interpretation was overwhelmingly loved by Haydn." (Gassner, *Universallexikon*, in which he is erroneously given as Zisler). Zistler, in the service of Count Erdödy, played at the Academy in 1772, in the theater next to the castle, and three times in the Academy of the *Tonkünstler Sozietät*; 1778-1786 he was concert master to Prince Batthyany in Bratislava, and is then mentioned as music director to Prince Grassalkovitz. He also participated in a concert of the singers Elisabeth and Franziska Distler. Schönfeld's *Jahrbuch der Tonkunst in Wien und Prag* calls Demuth and Eppinger excellent pupils of the late outstanding Zistler. According to the obituary, Zistler died on March 18, 1794, at the age of fifty (see Pohl, *Joseph Haydn* II, p. 101). Zistler played a part in the lodge "Zur Sicherheit," concerning which see Abafi V, p. 172. Besides Zistler, we find the following represented: Franz Edler von Hauslab, the Master of the lodge, the Deputy Master Udvarnovsky, the book dealer

138

Simon Peter Weber, orator of the lodge, and Georg Karl Zillagh. Zistler's entry reads as follows:

> *Der Tempel ist in dir*
> *den musst du selbsten weihen,*
> *wennst glücklich sein willst hier,*
> *Und ewigkeitens Reihen.* (?)

One of the most interesting entries is the Greek quotation written by Lorenz Leopold Haschka (1749-1827), who belonged to the St. Joseph lodge. The entry dates from Nov. 10, 1784, roughly the time of Mozart's initiation. Similarly to Hoffmann, Haschka was a spy and informer in the Craft. Rumor has it that he invested a sum presented him by Alxinger in the slave trade. In his dictionary, Gerber mentions a piano trio which appeared under Haschka's authorship. He is best known as the poet of the Austrian national anthem, *Gott erhalte Franz den Kaiser*. Whether Stephan Andreas Haslinger, whose entry is dated October 9, 1784, is related to the family of musicians and publishers, is unknown to me. (p. 28)

About the English masonic musicians cf. the appropriate articles in *Grove's Dictionary of Music and Musicians*. (p. 31)

Geminiani, Francesco Saverio, born 1679 or 1680, died 1762 in Dublin, famous as composer of concertos and sonatas, author of one of the first violin instruction books, *The art of playing on the violin*, which appeared anonymously in 1730. See the article on Geminiani by Franz Gigling in Blume, *Die Musik in Geschichte und Gegenwart*.

Concerning the Anacreontic Society, see Nettl, *National Anthems* (New York, 1952).

Lenz, *Hofrat* in Altenburg, 1717-1780, initiated into the lodge "Archimedes zu den drei Reissbrettern" in 1742. He edited his song book for that lodge and published a second, smaller collection in 1775. (p. 34)

Johann Gottlieb Görner (1697-1778). See Schering, *Johann Seb. Bach und das Musikleben Leipzigs im 18. Jahrhundert* (Leipzig, 1941).

Johann Valentin Görner (1702-1762), music director at the Hamburg cathedral. Reprint of his odes in vol. 57 of *Denkmäler deutscher Tonkunst*. See Friedländer, *Das deutsche Lied im 18. Jahrhundert* (Stuttgart, 1902) and Kretzschmar, *Geschichte des neuen deutschen Liedes* (1911). (p. 35)

Irmgard Leux, *Christian Gottlob Neefe* (Leipzig, 1925). (p. 37)

C. G. Telonius, an amateur in Hamburg who published several song collections and whose name appears in several Masonic song books (see Friedländer, I., p. 241). (p. 38)

Naumann was a member of the lodge "Zum goldenen Apfel" under whose auspices the songs of 1782 appeared. This refers to 36 songs composed by Weinlig, Seydelmann, Naumann, Schuster, Homilius (all from Dresden), and Tag. The preface indicates that the proceeds of the collection were to be used to alleviate suffering. The melodies, it says, had never been printed, and only some of the composers were masons. The lofty style of some of the songs, which is similar to Mozart's humanitarian style, shows that the composers, even the non-masons, had masonry in

139

mind. Thus, the "Fellow Craft's Song" by Schuster with its energetic unison eighths is appropriate to the Fellow Craft's initiation; *Bestimmung des Maurers* by Weinlig and *Wenn einst vom Staube losgerissen* by Tag are suited to the solemn atmosphere of the third degree. Naumann himself published *Vierzig Freymäurerlieder* under his own name in the same year. He designates them "for the use of German and French lodge dinners." The collection is dedicated to Prince Friedrich Wilhelm of Prussia. It does not show the strong side of Naumann. In 1780, J. F. Reichardt published an appendix, *Freymäurer-Lieder.* (p. 38)

Benjamin Franklin (1706-1790) became a mason in 1731 and in 1732 G. Warden of the Grand Lodge of Pennsylvania. In 1790 he appeared in England as a Mason, and in Paris he joined the famous scholarly lodge "Les 9 soeurs." He was Master of this lodge from 1779 to 1782; the 84 year old Voltaire entered the temple of this lodge supported by Franklin's arm. Franklin was the inventor of the glass harmonica, occupied himself with music and is supposed to have composed. It is by no means impossible for Franklin to have been the composer of the two masonic songs (see Nettl, in *Musical Quarterly,* 1930). (p. 40 Cf. Plate 4)

As a curiosity of cultural history we give a report of the masonic "horse comedy" reprinted by Abafi. It was directed by Brother Hyam, who had just arrived from London, in 1784: (p. 44)

"An opportunity was offered by the royal circus, opened in April 1784 by Brother Hyam, who had just arrived from London. The performances of the competent equestrians were appreciated by the aristocracy, and especially by the Hungarian and Galician guards. Especially applauded were the ladies, particularly the youthful second wife of the aging director, whose protector and sponsor was the Prince Dietrichstein. Among the art-loving ladies of Vienna, the son of Hyam's first marriage, 22 year old Charles Hyam, became most popular; he was not only an excellent equestrian, but also an Adonis and a Hercules. About this time, Prince Dietrichstein was confirmed as *Landes-Grossmeister* and the sale of his property, Proskau, to King Frederick II of Prussia was settled. For these two reasons the Prince arranged a festival dinner in his palace at the beginning of May, to which director Hyam and his beautiful wife were invited. Unfortunately the lady, who drank like a dragoon, became unwell and wished to go home, to which her husband did not agree. The Prince was gallant enough to take her home in his carriage. After two hours he re-appeared among his guests. Director Hyam, meanwhile, had incited the idea that some kind of masonic surprise should be prepared for the Prince on his name-day, as a token of thanks for the party. He was asked to prepare something which could be performed in his circus. Hyam agreed, under the condition that those brothers who rode horseback would participate. This they did. The plans were made, the roles rehearsed, the prospects for the performance were good. And the great day (June 24) arrived. The masonic pantomime, *Adonirams Tod,* composed and conducted by Brother Hyam and performed by several brothers, was staged.

"The characters and actors in the pantomime follow: King Solomon:

140

Hyam; Adoniram, architect of the temple: Johann, Count Esterhazy; the Queen of Sheba: Pottyondy, lieutenant and Hungarian guard; the three murderers: Danczkay, Doloviczényi, and Bacskády, lieutenants and Hungarian guards; finally, the retinue of King Solomon and the Queen of Sheba, priests of Baal, journeymen and apprentices in the construction of the temple, represented by: Báróczy and Sooky, both riding masters and 2nd sergeants of the guard in the Hungarian Guards; Wiesen, Bohuss, riding masters; Bourgeois, riding master and auditor of the Galician guards; Kauff, adjutant of the Toscana-infantry; Véghely, Bacsák, Majthényi, and Vass, lieutenants and Hungarian guards. All performers and spectators were masons, and the latter had to give the pass-word when entering. It is noteworthy that the entire pantomime was given on horseback, as a St. John's celebration by the lodge "Zur gekrönten Hoffnung." But all other Viennese lodges were also represented. The guests of honor sat on a special stage: Prince Dietrichstein, the provincial prefects Counts Stampa, Pálffy, and Bánffy; the district prefects Barons Kressl and Gebler. Of the lodge "Zur gekrönten Hoffnung," the following were present: Masters Paar and Matolay, the Second Steward Epstein, Treasurer Count Stockhammer, further First Lieutenant Székely, book dealer Gräffer, banker Gontard, art dealer Artaria, Dr. Ferro, court actor Adamberger, Lieutenant-Field Marshal Clerfait, the Counts Ernst and Dom. Kaunitz-Rietberg, J. Ried, cook to Count Esterhazy, and Sardagna, treasurer of the Cardinal-Archbishop of Vienna. Among the other guests there were various aristocrats, high government officials and officers, as well as notables of Viennese scholarship and art, including the famous Sonnenfels.

"The 'horse comedy'—as a contemporary rightly designates this silly pantomime—lasting from 7 to 8:30 P.M., pleased the Prince so much that he visited the Hyams after the performance, thanked them, and agreed to grant them a wish. Thereupon the couple pleaded with him to make their son, Charles Hyam, a mason, and to be his sponsor. At first the Prince declined, but finally he undertook the preparations. Count Paar went to the lodge in order to fetch the necessary equipment. Meanwhile, the circus was arranged as a lodge as well as was possible in the rush. Thereupon, the meeting was held on horseback. Charles Hyam was initiated on horseback and dismounted only for taking the symbolic steps.

"As *frère terrible* they used the Swiss giant Hans Klaus, against whose participation in the pantomime the brothers had at first protested; they were placated when Hyam proved, with a certificate, that the giant had served in a Swiss lodge. Brother Klaus was a real giant, his forefinger was four inches thick, and 'he could carry as much as two mules.' He sat on Hyam's strongest stallion, but was able to reach the floor with his toes. In the initiation he had to thunder with a large piece of tin and to 'make lightning' with rosin, which caused the stallion to shy and almost to throw him."

Cf. Brabbée, "Eine Loge zu Pferd," *Latomia* XXVII, pp. 277-288.

Röllig, regular visitor of the lodge "Zur Beständigkeit," famous virtuoso on the glass harmonica which had been perfected by Benjamin

Franklin in 1763. From 1764 to 1769, Röllig was music director of Ackermann's theatrical troupe in Hamburg and worked on improvements of the glass harmonica, the piano, and the piano-violin. After 1797 he worked at the Vienna Court Library until his death in 1804. G. Brabbée, in the article "Der Harmonikavirtuose Röllig," *Latomia* XXVII, pp. 257-267, tells the following phantastic tale: (p. 43)

"With his favorite instrument, the glass harmonica, he began making concert tours through Germany and France, and made his Vienna debut in 1781 with great success. Soon he was popular in Vienna and, in 1782, he joined a Masonic lodge. Then he was called to Paris, played at court, and became acquainted with Mesmer, in whose magnetic productions he participated. But he lost his appeal and had to travel in the smaller French towns. In one of these, probably Lyons, he fell seriously ill and was cured within two days by Cagliostro. After spending some time in Berlin and other German towns he returned to Vienna in 1785 and began to participate vigorously in Masonic activities. Without joining a lodge, he served all. At the St. John's feast, at initiations, memorial meetings, and dinners, he was always ready to entertain the brothers with his art. But his music affected his nerves, and, growing sickly, he eventually had to give up his art. Again he sought the help of Cagliostro, who was living in a house in Währing. But Röllig had lost confidence in Cagliostro's medicine, showed some of it to the Emperor's physician Störk, who, throwing the potion to the floor, himself undertook to cure Röllig. He was unsuccessful. The patient improved somewhat, but could not return to his art.

"He was obliged to find a new occupation. In his plight he turned to his brothers and, through Born, received an appointment as an official of the court library, which he held until his death in 1804. Röllig did not serve only the masons with his glass harmonica; magicians and other oddities made use of its fascinating sounds. Thus a certain Nefzer in Vienna asked him to come to his country house and to play for a few minutes at a given signal. Röllig agreed. They rode to the estate whose park, surrounded by a wall, Röllig found very beautiful. Temples, grottos, waterfalls, labyrinths, subterranean chambers, offered great variety. Left alone for a time, he was summoned by a servant who asked him to follow, but who hurried on, leaving Röllig to satisfy his curiosity.

"On the way he heard, coming from a basement, the muffled sound of trombones. Röllig hurried down the stairs and saw a vault in which a corpse was being placed into a coffin, to the accompaniment of funeral music. To one side was a man dressed in white, covered with blood, whose arm was being bandaged. Except for the helpers, all present were dressed in long, black cloaks and armed with swords. Skeletons, thrown in a heap, lay in the entrance of the vault, which was illuminated by the weird lights of oil flames. Frightened, he hurried back and was now led by the servant into the garden, which was lighted in green and looked like a fairyland.

"Röllig was posted behind an arbor whose inside was painted sky blue. Immediately an unconscious man was brought in, presumably the one whose arm had been bandaged; his companions were now splendidly dressed so that Röllig could not recognize them any more. At the signal, Röllig began to play, and the unconscious one, after a few minutes, awoke and asked 'where am I?' and 'whose voice am I hearing?' Loud jubilations and happy music were the answer. All took their swords and hurried with the unconscious one into the garden, leaving the musician to his own reflections. Röllig thought he had experienced a tale from the *Arabian Nights.*"

This story fits in with the notions about the fabulous effects of the glass harmonica which were current in that period. Goethe thought he heard in it the "heart's blood of the world." Röllig himself, in a fragment written in Berlin in 1787, says that the effect of the instrument was close to supernatural. If it were lost again, the legends about it would approach those of Orpheus's lyre (see Bruno Hoffmann in *Musik in Geschichte und Gegenwart*).

Joseph Bauernjöpel was *Hofkanzlist* at the book censorship commission and was active in literature. He was Master of the lodge "Beständigkeit," among whose members were the composer Joseph Blaske, evidently the violinist Joseph Blaschek who was a member of the orchestra of Count Esterhazy from 1769 to 1772; further, Ludwig Fischer, the basso who sang Osmin's role in the first performance of Mozart's *Entführung* in Mannheim. For this excellent singer, Mozart wrote the aria *Aspri rimorsi atroci* (K. 432). Perhaps Fischer, like Lange and Adamberger, worked for Mozart's initiation into the lodge. Abafi also names Franz Adam Mitscha among the members, but this man, a composer, cannot be the same as Franz Mitscha, music director to Count Questenberg in Jaromeritz, who had already died in 1745. (p. 44)

Tobias Phillip von Gebler (1726-1786), served the cause of culture and economics in the Habsburg empire. He was a member of the lodge "Zur wahren Eintracht." (p. 56)

Schikaneder was accepted into the lodge "Die Wachsende zu den 3 Schlüsseln." (p. 61)

Concerning Giesecke, see Otto Rommel, *Die altwiener Volkskomödie* (Vienna, 1952). (p. 63)

According to Lennhoff, Giesecke was initiated on St. John's day. According to Rommel, Giesecke was proud of his masonic membership, displayed his emblems frequently, used the sign below his signature, and owed his success partly to his masonic associations.

About the confused history of the sources for the *Magic Flute*, see also Komorzynski, *Der Vater der Zauberflöte* (Vienna, 1948), and "Die Zauberflöte und Dschinnistan," *Mozart-Jahrbuch*, 1954.

Wieland, Christoph Martin (1733-1813) had long been interested in Freemasonry. But his opinion fluctuated between recognition and rejection. At the age of 76 he applied for initiation to the lodge "Amalia," whose secretary was Archduke Karl August of Weimar, and whose master was Friedrich Justin Bertuch. In consideration of his age, he was initiated at a restricted meeting attended by Goethe. At Wieland's funeral, Goethe delivered a masonic address. (p. 69)

Mozart did not take the chorale *Ach Gott, vom Himmel sieh' darein* from a Protestant song book, but from Johann Philipp Kirnberger's *Die Kunst des reinen Satzes* (1774-1779). The second motif, with the chromatic sigh, is from the same work. As Wilhelm Fischer indicates in an essay ("Der, welcher wandelt diese Strasse voll Beschwerden," *Mozart-Jahrbuch*, 1950) this counter-motif is taken from a Kyrie of the *Missa S. Henrici* by Heinrich Biber. In a manner similar to Bach, this pacing bass line symbolizes the road, while the sighs represent the woes and hardships of this road. (p. 92)

"Sisters," according to masonic terminology, are the wives of those who, after initiation, are presented with a pair of white gloves by their spouses. (p. 93)

In the original libretto of 1791 a passage, stricken in later editions, seems to refer to the incipient persecution of masons: "Let prejudice find fault with us initiates. It affects wisdom and reason like a spider-web attacking a column. But malicious prejudice must go; and it will go as soon as Tamino himself grasps the greatness of our art."

Goethe's fragment appeared as the second part of the *Taschenbuch* of the year 1802 in Bremen, published by Friedrich Wilmans. The reprint of Vulpius' version of the *Magic Flute* appeared in 1908 with an introduction by Dr. Hans Löwenfeld. Its title page reads: "The Magic Flute, an opera in three acts. New arrangement. The Music is by Mozart. Weimar, printed with Glüsing's writings, 1794." It is likely that Vulpius (1762-1827), author of *Rinaldo Rinaldi,* was a mason. In his journal, *Curiositäten,* he repeatedly deals with the Knights Templar and the Rosicrucians. See also Nettl, *Goethe und Mozart* (Esslingen, 1949). (p. 94)

About Goethe and Freemasonry, see Dr. Hugo Wernekke, *Goethe und die königliche Kunst,* and the article in Lennhoff which cites nine definitely masonic poems. There are masonic allusions in *Wilhelm Meister,* in *Märchen,* and in the fragment *Geheimnisse;* the aberrations of Freemasonry are criticized in *Grosskophta.* Goethe was initiated into the "Amalia" lodge on June 23, 1780. A year later he was made Fellow Craft, and on March 2, 1782, he was raised to the third degree.

Bernhard Anselm Weber (1766-1821), an imitator of Gluck, who was also heard as a traveling virtuoso on the glass harmonica. His relationship to Röllig indicates his interest in the esoteric. (p. 96)

In Vulpius' version, the first verse of Sarastro's aria begins *In diesen heiligen Mauern,* the second, *In diesen heiligen Hallen.*

Concerning Goethe's continuation of the *Magic Flute,* see Victor Junk, *Goethes, Fortsetzung der Mozart'schen Zauberflöte* (Berlin, 1900). (p. 100)

INDEX

145

146

147

148

Sonnenfels, Joseph von, 10, 46, 118, 135, 136, 141
Sonnleithner, Leopold, 82, 87
Sousa, J. P., 129
Spaur, Count Friedrich and Family, 10, 11, 12, 133, 134
Sperontes (Johann Sigismund Scholze), 33, 34
Speyer, Wilhelm, 127
Spitta, Philipp, 34
Spohr, Ludwig, 127
Springer, Vinzent, 18
Stadler, Anton, 18, 21
Star-Spangled Banner, 31
Steenstrupp, K. J. V., 63
Steffan, J. A., 118
Stollberg, Count, 10
Storace, Steven and Nancy, 25, 124
Süssmayr, Franz Xaver, 22, 121
Summer, Wenzel, Chaplain, 15
Swift, Jonathan, 5
Symbolism, 6, 88 ff.

Taskin, Henri Josephe, 40
Telonius, C. G., 38, 139
Terrasson, Jean, Abbé, 69 ff., 88
Thackeray, W. M., 79
Tinti, Bartholomäus and Anton von, 17, 135
Tomaschek, Wenzel, 97
Trattner, Theresia von, 25
Treitschke, Georg Friedrich, 66, 67

Ungar, Raphael, 20, 137
Unterberger, Ignaz, 13, 49, 51, 137
Udvarnoky, Br., 138

van Swieten, Gottfried, 22, 135
Veidl, Theodor, 128
Vignet, de, Physician, 45
Vignoles, de, 32
Viotti, Jean Battiste, 41
Vitzthum, Ignaz, 32
Voltaire, F. M. A., 118, 119

Vulpius, Christian August, 94, 95, 144

Wagner, Richard, 35, 112, 128
"Wahre Eintracht," (Lodge), 13, 14, 15, 16, 17, 25, 28, 43, 46, 50, 53, 135
"Wahrheit," (Lodge), 16
"Wahrheit und Einheit," (Lodge), Prag, 20, 49, 137
Wappler, Christian Friedrich, 50
Washington, George, 5
Weber, Aloysia, 103, 122, 123
Weber, B. A., 144, 58
Weber, Simon Peter, 139
Webbe, Samuel, 32
Weber, Br. ("Wahre Eintracht"), 139
Wegeler, Franz Gerhard, 127
Weinbrenner, Joseph von, 18, 19, 136
Weisse, Felix Christian, 118
Weissegger, Prof., 28
Weisshaupt, Adam, 9, 10, 133
Wernekke, Hugo, 144
Wesley, Samuel, 31
Wetzlar, Raimund, 125
Whiteman, Paul, 129
Wieland, Ch. M., 3, 5, 14, 65, 67 ff., 78, 118, 143
Wiesinger, Albert, 85
Winter, Peter von, 66, 98, 100
Winterstein, Alfred, 132
"Wohltätigkeit," Lodge, 14, 15, 17, 26, 47, 49, 54, 111, 135
Wolfegg, Count Anton, 11, 133
Wranitzsky, Paul, 18, 42, 43, 49, 68, 95
Wyzewa and St. Foix, 48

Zauner, Franz, 14
Zellweker, Edwin, 134
Zelter, Karl Friedrich and Adelheid, 95
Ziegenhagen, Franz Heinrich, 55
Ziegler, Marianne, 25
Zillagh, Georg Karl, 139
Zille, Moritz Alexander, 83
Zistler, Joseph, 26, 138, 139
Zöhrer, Franz, 42
"Zorobabel," Lodge, Copenhagen, 36

149

ACKNOWLEDGMENT

I am indebted to the following persons who were helpful with translations and editorial work: Mrs. Robert Gold, London, who made the first English draft, Dr. Alexander von Gode, Mr. Charles Shapiro and my son, Dr. Bruno Nettl, Detroit, who is responsible for the final version. I am most grateful to Mr. Siegfried Mamerow and Dr. Dagobert Runes, who made the publication of this book possible. I also have to express my deep appreciation to my wife, Margaret von Gutfeld-Nettl for her permanent assistance. Finally, Mr. Thomas Atcherson was helpful in reading the proofs.

P. N.